THE U.S. NAVY-CURTISS FLYING BOAT NC-4

THE U.S. NAVY-CURTISS FLYING BOAT NC-4

AN ACCOUNT OF THE FIRST TRANSATLANTIC FLIGHT

RICHARD V. SIMPSON

FONTHILL

Dedicated to the Memory of Irene V.
My sweet, gentle wife and best friend for fifty-five years.

Fonthill Media Language Policy

Fonthill Media publishes in the international English language market. One language edition is published worldwide. As there are minor differences in spelling and presentation, especially with regard to American English and British English, a policy is necessary to define which form of English to use. The Fonthill Policy is to use the form of English native to the author. Richard V. Simpson was born and educated in the United States and now lives at Bristol RI, therefore American English has been adopted in this publication.

Fonthill Media Limited
Fonthill Media LLC
www.fonthillmedia.com
office@fonthillmedia.com

First published in the United States of America
and the United Kingdom 2016

British Library Cataloguing in Publication Data:
A catalogue record for this book is available from the British Library

ISBN 978-1-62545-009-8

Typeset in 10.5pt on 13pt Sabon
Printed and bound in England

Preface

United States Senate
Congressional Record
July 16, 1986.
First across the Atlantic in 1919.
Senator Claiborne Pell, D-RI

Mr. Pell

Mr. President, Charles A. Lindbergh is justly remembered and honored as the first man to make a solo nonstop flight across the Atlantic Ocean in 1927. Less known is the flight of the U.S. Navy's *NC-4* flying boat which crossed from Newfoundland to Lisbon, Portugal with stops in the Azores Islands in May 1919.

The honor of accomplishing the first flight across the Atlantic belongs to the U.S. Navy, the *NC-4*, and its designers and builders.

Glenn H. Curtiss, the inventor of the flying boat, had worked at the Navy's Bureau of Construction on the development of ocean-going planes and then had formed his own plant in Hammondsport, N.Y. The Curtiss plant subcontracted many of the planes' components in order that they might be complete on time; one of the subcontractors was the Herreshoff Manufacturing Co. of Bristol, R.I. which built the hulls for many flying boats.

The flight of the big Navy flying boats began on May 2, 1919, with the formation of the NC Seaplane Division One (N equals Navy, C equals Curtiss). On May 8, 1919, a squadron of three Navy Curtiss [float planes] went on a one thousand mile test flight from Rockaway, New York to Newfoundland which was the established departure point for the Transatlantic crossing. Other aviators spurred on by the London *Daily Mail* offer of £10,000 pounds prize money for the first to cross the Atlantic were gathering at Newfoundland waiting for clear weather. At about 6 p.m. on Friday, May 16, the three Navy planes took off for the Azores, the first challengers to leave Newfoundland. A member of the Navy ground crew was the late Charles Callan of Bristol, R.I.

The *NC-1* and the *NC-3* had difficulty on the flight to the Azores. Because of the fog, the *NC-1* touched down in the water but could not take off again in bad weather. The waves destroyed enough of her hull to eventually cause her to sink, but luckily her crew was rescued.

The *NC-3* also put down in the water and unable to fly because of damage to the engine ended her journey at Ponta Delgada, Sao Miguel, in the Azores.

The *NC-4* had better luck, under the command of the navigator, Lt. Comdr. Albert C. Read; the crew consisted of Lt. Elmer Stone, U.S. Coast Guard; pilot Lt. Walter Hinton; co-pilot Ens. Herbert C. Rodd; radio officer Lt. James L. Breese; engineer and Chief Machinist's Mate Eugene S. Rhodes.

On Saturday, May 17, after a flight of 15 hours and13 minutes, the *NC-4* touched down in the harbor of Horta, Fayal, in the Azores. Sunday's newspaper headlines in America treated it as a victory because the plane was safely in a Portuguese port. The *NC-4* was grounded at Fayal for 9 days by the fog. On the morning of May 27, the *NC-4* flew eastward to Lisbon and after a flight of 9¾ hours became the first plane to conquer the Atlantic. In the space of 19 days, the *NC-4* and its crew had travelled 3,322 miles in 41 hours and 58 minutes in the air.

The reception in Lisbon was tumultuous and lasted for 3 days; 21-gun salutes were fired and the Tagus River resounded with the ringing of church bells. The Portuguese government awarded the fliers the Grand Cross of the Order of the Tower and Sword. On May 30, the *NC-4* left for Plymouth, England in order that the trip might end at the site of the Pilgrim's departure nearly 300 years before in 1620.

To commutate this landmark flight the Navy has planned a recreation of the flight of the *NC-4* during this summer. Representatives of the Government of the United States and Portugal will be on hand at festivities honoring the Navy for its seldom celebrated accomplishment. I know this reenactment flight will be of great interest in my own state of Rhode Island where so many of our citizens are descended from residents of the Azores and Portugal. And Rhode Island can take particular pride in the fact that the Herreshoff Manufacturing Co. of Bristol, R.I. played a major role in contributing to the successful flight—the first to conquer the Atlantic.

Contents

Acknowledgments

Once again special thanks are extender to Herreshoff Marine Museum's Archivist/ Liberian Noreen Rickson for painstakingly searching her records for relevant *NC-4* documents for use in this narrative.

Author's Note

My interest in the Navy–Curtiss flying boats became aroused when I learned the hull of the *NC-4* was built in my home town—Bristol, Rhode Island—by the Herreshoff Manufacturing Company.

Curtiss subcontracted the fuselage work of the first pod of four NCs. The *NC-4* hull work was subcontracted to the Herreshoff Manufacturing Company with the proviso that construction would be done in the same manner as the Herreshoff was known to apply to their swift and sturdy sailing craft. A wood fuselage built just like a boat hull was constructed at the Bristol yard in 1918.

As I later learned, building seaplane hulls for the Navy was not unusual for Herreshoff. The company had previously built twenty hulls of various proportions and configurations beginning in 1902. However, the *NC-4* hull was special, it was forty-five feet long and ten feet abeam, it had to be especially strong to withstand the impact of landing and taking off at sea; it also had to be lightweight and watertight.

To accomplish contract specifications, a double layer of Sitka spruce planking fastened with copper was laid at opposing forty-five degree angles from a Sitka spruce keel. Between the planking Herreshoff's yacht mechanics stretched a layer of muslin in marine glue. When complete the hull weighed only 2,800 pounds.

After a devastating fire, the *NC-2* was salvaged to repair the *NC-1* and the leftovers became spare parts for the *NC-4*.

During the run-up to the actual take-off for the much-heralded transatlantic flight, the *NC-4* was plagued by multiple mishaps. All the NCs including the *NC-4* were snowed under by mechanical problems of one sort or another including damage from storm and fire but only the feisty *NC-4* completed the goal of a transatlantic flight.

Because of the many hard luck events plaguing the *NC-4*, national newspaper writers were calling the *NC-4* the "lame duck", circulating ill-founded reports that she would be scratched from the transatlantic flight. Because we know the end to this saga, it proves that news-writers are poor prognosticators.

The facts concerning the build up and actual flight of the NCs is taken from several sources. In an effort to make this narrative the definitive document on the subject, I chose to glean the most in-depth facts from long forgotten articles written by authors who were closest to the days of the premier transatlantic flight.

. . . . .

A problem that many writers and fine art painters experience, is knowing when to stop. With this narrative I was tempted to include a plethora of interesting facts which would not necessarily advance knowledge about the NC flying boats. Because I am a nonfiction writer and a painter, I know when I have written enough about a subject—so, I stopped.

Introduction

The song, "Those daring young men in their flying machines" certainly does apply to those courageous aviators: pilots, navigators and crews who dared attempt the first transatlantic voyage in the world's first generation of large flying boats—eight years before Lindbergh's solo flight.

The U.S. Navy got its first "aeroplane" in 1911, the Curtiss A-1, single-engine pusher; constructed of cloth, balsawood and bailing wire, it was lightweight and fragile. The first Navy pilot to master the rudimentary controls of the machine was Lt. Theodore G. Ellyson.

Airplanes take off and they land, sometimes successfully, sometimes not. What makes this tale so dramatic is conflict, difficulties, accidents and even failure.

Just as the Curtiss JN became known as the "Jenny," jointly designed by the Navy and Curtiss during the First World War, the NC series of flying boats was christened "Nancy." This history of the "Nancy Boats" and Seaplane Division One delivers full force all of the trials and triumphs of the effort.

The NC craft was planned as an anti-submarine weapon, which was sturdy enough to fly across the Atlantic for use in France. Too late for war service, the entire fleet of three Navy NCs attempted the first transatlantic crossing in 1919, with the *NC-4*, the solitary survivor, landing in Britain on May 31. The craft made the journey by flying, floating, and boating its way across the Atlantic.

Overshadowed because of its proximity to the end of the First World War and subsequent milestone flights, the flight of the NC flying boats is now only a bare statistical footnote in record books. Today, there are few who are aware of the significance of the first successful transatlantic flight.

The first gaggle of Navy–Curtiss airplanes became operational too late to be of consequence in the First World War. However, the United States Navy decided to dramatize its tremendous range of power by making the first transatlantic flight with four of the new flying boats.

Navy brass made every effort to give the flight the character of a carefully planned military operation rather than a theatrical show unworthy of the attention of admirals. Navy tacticians concerned for the safety of crews and machines dictated that the planes would fly as a squadron, each with a navigator, two pilots, a radioman and two engine specialists. Each craft carried communications equipment, a transmitter which could send a distress signal, and a radio compass which is designed to give bearings to the navigator.

Another instrument on board keeping the planes on course was a special sextant designed by future Antarctic explorer Commander Richard E. Byrd. The Byrd sextant consists of a bubble in a tube creating an artificial horizon making observations possible above clouds. He also invented a drift meter, which used a flair or smoke bomb dropped on the sea to calculate the wind force and direction. Special charts were drawn which cut the time of computation from observations, a reliable time-saving shortcut.

After weeks of tests and mishaps, three NCs with five- and six-man crews finally lifted off. Lieutenant Patrick Bellinger commanded the *NC-1*, Commander Jack Towers skippered the *NC-3* and Lieutenant Commander. Albert C. Read was captain of the *NC-4*.

On May 8, 1919, *NC-1*, *-3*, and *-4* took off from Naval Air Station Rockaway, Long Island, New York, with Trepassey, Newfoundland, the intermediate stop prior to their attempt at crossing the Atlantic. After delays from *NC-4*'s engine trouble near Cape Cod and bad weather at Trepassey, all three aircraft finally departed on their grueling Atlantic crossing on Friday evening, May 16. In contrast to the present, these aircraft flew at a maximum speed of 90 mph, with the crews exposed to the elements in open, unheated cockpits. To reach a scheduled stop for fuel in the Azores required more than 17 hours elapsed flying time; the entire crossing would add up to more than 26 hours!

In his August 1961, *National Geographic* article, Vice Admiral P. N. L. Bellinger, (ret.) writes:

> Of course, we knew where Europe was, but finding it meant trusting new navigation instruments never used on a long-distance flight before. Ships spaced along the route flashed guiding signals, but *NC-1* lost its bearing in a fog. We grouped and circled, sometimes skimming the tops of waves, and finally gave up. Our pilots, Lt. Louis T. Barin and Lt-Cdr. Marc A. Mitscher, later a hero of the war in the Pacific, brought us down safely, despite heavy seas.
>
> Fraught by engine trouble and inclement weather, *NC-1* and *-3* landed short of the Azores, but with high seas and waves cresting over 20 feet, we were unable to take off again. Yet, *NC-3* sailed and taxied backwards some 250 miles to the Azores, a formidable adventure in its own right!
>
> *NC-1* was abandoned to the sea, the crew being rescued by a Greek freighter. The *NC-4*, after what seemed like impossible delays in weather, engine repairs, and other problems, finally made Lisbon, Portugal, on May 27, becoming the first aircraft to cross the Atlantic.

Commander Ted Wilbur recounts a few memories of the historic flight in his 1969 memoir:

Judging by the background, I believe this series of six snapshots were taken at Trepassey Bay, Newfoundland.

In this photo, Commander Read is not visible in the navigator's forward cockpit; he may have ducked down into the hull to speak to his crew.

We can thank an alert amateur photographer for capturing these rare images of the *NC-4* powering-up his engines for a high speed pre-take off run.

The photographer is unflinching as the roaring monster machine rushes close to him, then passing and begins to become airborne.

Pilot Walter T. Hinton has "the pedal to the metal" as the powerful engines push the flying boat across the water throwing up a billowing rooster-tail.

The author purchased these photos at a Massachusetts flea market in the mid-1970s.

The *NC-4* was the first in 1919. Its place in history and the significance of its flight have long been diminished by the public's love of contemporary heroics. The crews were soon forgotten as America looked to peace and prosperity after the war. This disdain is best demonstrated by our Congress, which took more than 10 years to appropriate the meager budget needed to authorize and award special medals for the NC crews.

May 17, 1919, started off as a bleak day on the Islands of the Vultures. With classical whaling, Nantucket-style, one of their chief industries, the inhabitants of the Portuguese Azores were long accustomed to watching the sea. To this day, upon the lush green slopes and mountainsides are watchers' huts, shelters for the anxious eyes that seek a wispy spout, poised below, among the rocks of lack and bights, whalers wait, boats and harpoons at the ready, eager for the signal that monsters are at hand. Now radio is used, but back then, once the telltale plume was spotted, fires were ignited in line with where the prey was seen to "blow."

However, on that morning, there were no guiding lights; the mid-Atlantic pinnacles were misty with the shrouds of fog. Among rocky promontories, drizzle pierced low-lying clouds. A murky, thickening overcast had settled on the archipelago and, for a whale watcher, prospects of sighting blue-gray beasts were dim indeed.

Before noon, visibility on the island of Fayal was reduced to one or two miles. A west wind swept foggy blankets onto the southern shores, while turbulent air, spilling down from the mountains created a sporadic breeze along the coast. There, on the Bay of Praia, shortly after 11:00 a.m., a strange sighting was made.

Observers on the beach said it started with a sound, a growing hum, a growling noise from seaward. Suddenly, as they peered toward Joao Diaz Point, from out of the gloom, slicing across the waters a huge gray shape appeared: a whale-like body seemingly attached to burnished appendages that flickered dully in the half-light. Wallowing in an arching turn, the "monster" barked, sputtered, then emitted a tremendous roar and, as quickly as it had appeared, faded away in the sound of thunder.

As startled farmers and fishermen hastened from the scene, never again to experience so fantastic a sight; 20,000 pounds of wood, metal, fabric and fuel were plunging into the damp air and making round the next peninsula. Just beyond, in the harbor of Fayal's capital city, Horta, lay the warship, the USS *Columbia*.[1] At 11:23 a.m., an entry was made in the ship's log: "Sighted *NC-4* abreast Espalamaca Point."

A quivering wake spread across the Bay of Praia, mute testimony that for the first time an aircraft had flown from the American continent to a European shore.

1

Historic Perspective

Early in May 1919, U.S. Navy Captain N. E. Irwin arrived at Rockaway Beach, New York carrying a handful of four-leaf clovers. He distributed them to the six-man crews of the three NC flying boats about to tackle the challenging Atlantic.

. . . . .

On wings of wood and filmy fabric, the United States Navy entered the era of motorized flight—that memorable event happened in 1911. In March, Congress appropriated the princely sum of $25,000 for research and development of naval aviation. The initial aeroplane purchased by the United States cost the treasury $5,500; this first purchase was the Curtiss *A-1*, the first of tens of thousands of aircraft acquired over the following century by the three branches of sea services—Navy, Marine Corps and Coast Guard.

At the beginning of the United States Navy's serious interest in aviation, one man was in the forefront of the country's aircraft industry—Glenn H. Curtiss. His design and construction facilities in Hammondsport, New York dwarfed all his competitors, including the Wright Company. Lieutenant Theodore G. Ellyson was the first naval officer detailed to flight training at the Curtiss factory, which was in the summer of 1911. Ellyson has the distinction of being designated Naval Aviator No. 1. After some basic training, Ellyson joined Curtiss in test flying the *A-1* and the *A-2* flying boats from Lake Keuka in New York's Finger Lakes region.

Soon after, the Navy detailed two additional officers for training. Lieutenant John Rogers went to the Wright School in Dayton, Ohio and Lieutenant John H. Towers joined Ellyson at the Curtiss factory. Towers learned on a Wright designed and built landplane, the *A-3*, which was later modified as a "hydroaeroplane" fitted with pontoons.

These three Navy officers, Ellyson, Rogers and Towers, were the first of the many thousands of men who would wear the service's distinctive gold wings.

The U.S. Navy's first group of "flyboys" was young, newly minted junior

Curtiss and U.S. Navy Aviator No.1 Lieutenant Theodore G. Ellyson sit at the dual controls of an experimental biplane, *c.* 1911.

officers—1903 and 1906 graduates from the Naval Academy. Ellyson and Rogers also served in submarines, indicating extraordinary adaptability.

The Congress funded construction of eight new battleships from 1910 to 1912, and others were on the drawing board; the Navy was not going to scrap its battleship and cruiser plans for construction of a new fangled flattop for the unproven idea that airplanes can take off and land on a ship at sea. Therefore, most early Navy airplanes featured pontoon floats and fuselage built in the shape of a boat hull.

The December 7, 1912 issue of the weekly *Aero and Hydro* magazine published the following article about Glenn H. Curtiss' new flying boat.

> The new flying boat built by Glenn H. Curtiss for the War Department has completed the official tests before the board of army officers appointed to observe the trials. The climbing test which required a climb of 150 feet per minute was accomplished November 27, when the machine rose to an altitude of 1200 feet in 6½ minutes.
>
> The speed trial was the first to be undertaken and was accomplished successfully. The aeroplane was driven six times over a measured course three times in each direction and the speed taken by an observer from flag signals at the start and finish. The average speed was 58.4 miles per hour. There was a 10-mile wind blowing at the time diagonal

> to the course. In calm the speed would have been several miles per hour faster, but the machine is well above the requirement which is 45 miles per hour.
>
> In the two-hour test a total weight of 900 pounds was carried. Aviator Wildman was accompanied by John D. Cooper, another Curtiss aviator on the trial. J. Lansing Callan was a passenger on the speed and climbing trials.
>
> Lieutenants McLeary, Brereton and Park, who constituted the board have expressed themselves well satisfied with the performance of the machine and recommended its immediate acceptance.
>
> The aeroplane is of the latest flying boat type and has many features especially designed for military requirements. The engine is fitted with a starting device so that it may be stopped and started again while the machine is in the water. This is the first of the flying boats to be used for military purposes.
>
> The flying boat built for the United States Army which passed the speed and duration tests last week will now be shipped to San Diego for use at the army's winter camp.
>
> The boat climbed 1600 feet in less than 15 minutes carrying a load of 600 pounds. In making the test for duration last week the boat was supposed to carry only 600 pounds, but through some mistake almost 300 pounds extra was put on so that the test was made while carrying a load of nearly 900 pounds.
>
> The flying boat built for the United States Navy was put through all of the tests required by the government this week. It passed the speed, duration, quick climbing and turning tests without a hitch of any sort. After a few of the fittings have been adjusted slightly and the muffler altered to suit the officers it will be delivered to them for use in Cuba this winter. Lieutenant Ellyson and Naval Constructor Richardson acted as the official observers for the government at the trials. Francis Wildman operated the boat and Harvey Kays, one of the students at the [Curtiss School of Aviation] was his passenger.

The U.S. Marine Corps became active in aviation in 1912; Lieutenants Alfred A. Cunningham and Bernard L. Smith became the Corps first aviators. Marines' wartime duties included antisubmarine search patrols and instructing pilot recruits with the intricateness of piloting an aircraft. Two Marine pilots were awarded Medals of Honor for their actions with six-squadrons of the *DH-4* Bombing Group operating from France and Belgium.

In 1914, an unexpected opportunity to exhibit the ability of airplanes for surveillance and attack came when a dispute arose south of the border; American sailors on leave became entangled in a misunderstanding with Mexican soldiers. A confrontation ensued leading to a six-month occupation of the Mexican Port of Veracruz. Washington sent a detachment of six Navy aircraft in support of the Army and Marine occupying troops. On one mission, a civilian photographer was aboard snapping photos of the Mexican positions around the Port.

Naval air power progressed, when in 1915, a catapult was installed on the cruiser *North Carolina*.[1]

More noteworthy, Curtiss began building larger and more powerful flying boats. In 1917, when America entered the war the Model H *America* was the country's only twin-engine airplane. The following year, Curtiss' trimotor the *HS-21* with a 92-foot wing span and the ability to stay airborne for six-hours was flying long-range submarine search patrols. The *HS-21* was a serious advancement in American airpower.

By March 1918, Navy aviation was in the thick of aerial combat. Ensign Steven Potter destroyed an enemy seaplane off the coast of Germany, and Ensign John McNamara attacked a surfaced German U-boat—this being the first recorded aerial attack on a submarine. Lieutenant (jg) David S. Ingallis, flying a British bi-wing Sopwith Camel fighter, won his Ace designation after making his sixth-kill, a German Fokker D- VII.

In October 1918, Lieutenant Ralph Talbert with Corporal Robert G. Robertson, occupying the second seat as an observer, in a Marine squadron of *DH-4* bombers, flying over Belgium were intercepted by Fokkers and Pfalzers. Talbert and Robertson became separated from the squadron having to out-fly and out-shoot their way free of the enemy planes. Though seriously wounded, Robertson cleared and reloaded his Lewis machine gun with his uninjured arm and continued fighting. Later they claimed three definite and one possible kill.

With the end of the First World War, America experienced an inevitable downsizing of its military. Dedicated aviators continued however, to promote airpower with the public. For the curious public the most welcomed and entreating promotions was the barnstorming air shows.

The Navy planned to develop a long-range bomber capable of a transatlantic flight to support allies. The Curtiss H model was first considered, but development of the NC flying boat with four Liberty engines supplying surplus energy, translating into useful load carrying ability, won the day. By any standard, the NCs were large aircraft; they were the veritable giants of the day.

Eventually the day arrived for the three NC flying boats to take off on their unpredicted transatlantic voyage. Of the three, only the *NC-4* completed the mission taking 27 hours of flying time over 11 days, but the point had been made; naval aviation had ocean-spanning potential. The three heavily loaded planes under Commander John H. Towers (elevated to the rank of Admiral during the Second World War), went into the surf at Rockaway Beach at 10 a.m. on May 8, 1919. There were few spectators at the historic event because the public had grown weary of the frequent launch postponements. The few military and civilians present watched the cumbersome monster crafts taxi into Jamaica Bay and take off. They climbed slowly to 500 feet and set course for the northeast.

Weighing over 14-tons—when fully loaded and with a wingspan of 126-feet—they were the heaviest craft yet flown. The wooden hull was both a boat and a cramped cabin for the crew. The spruce hull was reinforced, to Navy specifications, hoping it would stand up to the pounding of heavy seas in case of an emergency ocean landing. The tail was held in place by booms from the hull and superstructure. Each plane had four 400 horsepower Liberty engines; one, a pusher, was right behind the center-forward engine.

In 1914, Keuka Lake was the scene of the testing of a Curtiss advanced float plane he called the *America. [Photo courtesy of American Heritage]*

In 1917, when the United States entered the war the Curtiss Model H *America* was the country's only twin-engine airplane. The *America* was sold to England as a prototype for 50 patrol seaplanes.

Indeed, not until 1922, did the Navy's first flat top come into being; she is the converted collier, the *Jupiter*. The ship received her flat top at the Norfolk Navy Yard where a short-narrow wooden flight deck and an aircraft elevator were installed, when commissioned in 1922; she was named the USS *Langley* (AV-3). In 1937, the *Langley* saw service as a seaplane tender and aircraft ferry. After 20 years of service to the U.S. Navy she was attacked on 27 February 1942 off the coast of Java by dive bombers of the Japanese 21st and 23rd Naval Air Flotillas and so badly damaged that she had to be scuttled by her escorts.

The USS *Langley* (CV-1) at Pearl Harbor, Oahu, Hawaiian Islands with 34 planes on her flight deck, May, 1928. Though newer, larger and faster aircraft carriers arrived in the fleet in the late1920s, the old "Covered Wagon" remained operational until October 1936, when she became converted to a seaplane tender and reclassified AV-3. *[USN]*

2

Glenn Hammond Curtiss (1878–1930)

A self-made man with only an eighth-grade education and without family wealth as a cushion, Curtiss's intelligence and inventive vision propelled him into the realm of the most respected pioneer in the field of aviation. He invented the first practical seaplane and flying boat and taught the United States Navy how to get off the ocean and into the air. He was a leading light in aircraft construction, engines and control systems and he led America into the industry of aviation.

Curtiss began his career as a bicycle mechanic and racer, earning fame as one of the leading cycle racers in western New York State. Daring to push the envelope for greater speed, he began building lightweight internal combustion engines for motorcycles. By 1903, Curtiss was one of Hammondsport's leading businessmen. He built and marketed his bicycles and motorcycles from his G. H. Curtiss Manufacturing Company.

In 1904 Curtiss entered the aeronautics field. He was propelled into that arena when the American aeronaut Thomas Scott Baldwin purchased a Curtiss motorcycle engine to power his airship the *California Arrow*. In 1907, at the invitation of Alexander Graham Bell, Curtiss joined the newly formed Aerial Experiment Association (AEA), flying his AEA *June Bug* from Hammondsport, New York. On January 23, 1907 he earned the title of being "the fastest man on earth," when he attained a speed of 136.3 mph aboard a motorcycle of his design.

Joseph Pulitzer's *New York World* offered a prize of $10,000 to the first aviator to follow the course of the Hudson River from New York to Albany, a distance of 152 miles, in a mechanically propelled airship. Curtiss, of course, was up to the challenge. He built a plane destined to carry him on his most impressive flight. He named the craft the *Hudson Flyer;* his goal was the longest and most dangerous cross-country flight yet attempted in the United States. It is not recorded that Curtiss broke a smile when presented the *World's* check in May 1910—but it is likely that he did.

Curtiss pioneered the design and operation of the superior American flying boats. His aircraft were the first to takeoff (1910) and a land (1911) from the deck of a warship. The idea of a hydroplane fascinated Curtiss, tinkering with the idea in the back of his head since his days with Bell's AEA group when he considered the scheme of turning the *June Bug* into a "water bug." It was the autumn of 1910,

In this *c.* 1909 photo, Curtiss is displaying his characteristic quiet intensity at the control wheel of one of his innovative flying machines. *[Photo is courtesy of American Heritage]*

On January 18, 1911 Eugene Ellyson touched down at 40 miles per hour on the *Pennsylvania's* improvised flight deck his wings barely clearing the crouching deck hands. Three hooks on the undercarriage of the plane snagging ropes stretched between sandbags brought the plane to a stop. *[USN]*

Dubbed "Old Covered Wagon" by aviators, the USS *Langley* (CV-1, later AV-3), a 11,500–ton aircraft carrier was a converted collier, the USS *Jupiter* (Collier 3) beginning in 1920. Commissioned in March 1922, the *Langley* was the U.S. Navy's first aircraft carrier. In October and November 1922, she launched, recovered and catapulted her first aircraft during operations in Atlantic and Caribbean waters training a generation of pilots. *[USN]*

when the United States Navy began considering an aviation arm of the service, this during the same time-frame as Curtiss's interest in designing a high-powered, sea-going flying boat.

> In charge of the looking [U.S. Navy investigation] was Captain Washington Irving Chambers, an innovative, forward-thinking [young] officer. Chambers sought to impress the navy brass by staging the takeoff of an airplane from a warship. Wilber Wright turned down the idea as being too risky, but Curtiss' pilot Theodore Ellyson was willing. On November 14, in Hamptons Roads off the Virginia coast, he cranked up the *Hudson Flyer* and sped down a wooden platform built over the forecastle of the cruiser *Birmingham*. The *flyer* lurched over the bow, clipped the wave tops and struggled into the air. This date is celebrated as the birth of naval aviation.
>
> Stephen W. Sears

After this successful experiment, Curtiss contacted Secretary of the Navy George von L. Meyer informing him that he was establishing a winter experimental station in California to investigate the adaptability of aeronautic science for military application. Always an astute businessman as well as inventor, he suggested to Secretary Meyer his intention to give free pilot training to any naval officer he would care to assign to his pilot training school. In January 1911, Lieutenant Theodore G. Ellyson,[2] formally of the navy submarine service, reported to the aviation flying school. Curtiss chose San Diego's North Island for his experimental station.

Before Curtiss began looking into the problem of designing a seaplane, he, Chambers and Ellyson plotted another spectacular exhibit for Navy brass. A wooden platform was cobbled together over the quarterdeck of the cruiser *Pennsylvania* anchored in San Francisco Harbor. With arresting gear of ropes stretched across the platform anchored with sandbags, on January 18, Ellyson made history by becoming the first pilot to land an airplane on a warship's deck. The *Pennsylvania's* skipper invited Ellyson to lunch with him and the ship's senior officers; after lunch, Ellyson flew off into the wild blue without mishap. Ellyson's daring flights initiated a productive partnership between the Navy and Curtiss; a practical seaplane had not yet been developed, but Curtiss managed to do it in less than two weeks—it was superb tinkering of the highest order.

On January 26, 1911, Curtiss prepared his new seaplane for a test flight, he taxied away from the beach, he applied full throttle, soared over the water and into the air. The next step was inventing retractable landing gear resulting in the first

Curtiss flying boat AB-3 shoots from a permanent catapult built on the stern of the armored cruiser USS *North Carolina* in 1916, becoming the first fighting ship equipped to carry and launch aircraft while at sea.

amphibian; the following year he designed a boat hull on which he could mount an engine and wings—thus inventing the world's first flying boat.

With the approach of the First World War, Curtiss emerged as a major supplier of flying boats to the United States Navy and allied European governments. He was a leading producer of aircraft engines, notably the famous OX-5. The Curtiss JN-4, the so-called "Jenny," was the standard training and all-purpose aircraft in American military service during the years prior to U.S. entry into the First World War.

As you will discover in this narrative, the Curtiss flying boat— the multi-engine *NC-4*, nick-named the "Nancy Boat" made the first flight across the Atlantic Ocean in 1919, opening the great era of long-distance flight that would mark the years between the two world wars.

On July 23, 1930, following surgery for acute appendicitis, Glenn H. Curtiss died of a pulmonary embolism. He was fifty-two years old.

3

The Challenge

Following the U.S. Navy's interest in aviation and flying boats in particular, the Navy Board sent an advisor to the Curtiss plant at Hammondsport, New York. The advisor was a young officer—Lieutenant John H. Towers—who later became Naval Aviator Number 3. Towers learned to fly under the tutelage of Glenn Curtiss and Lt. Theodore G. Ellyson, and as time went on they became close friends. Towers qualified as a pilot in August 1911, flying the Navy's first airplane, a Curtiss A-1 seaplane. Towers next traveled to North Island in San Diego, California where, in conjunction with the Curtiss Flying School, he took part in developing and improving naval aircraft types. On May 8, 1913, Lt. Towers flew a long-distance flight of 169 miles in a Curtiss flying boat from the Washington Navy Yard down the Potomac River and then up the Chesapeake Bay to the U.S. Naval Academy at Annapolis, Maryland. On June 20, 1913, Towers was nearly killed in an aviation mishap over the Chesapeake Bay. While he was flying as a passenger in a Wright seaplane, his plane was caught in a sudden downdraft and plummeted earthward. The pilot, Ensign W. D. Billingsley, was thrown from the aircraft and killed, becoming the first naval aviation fatality. Towers also was wrenched from his seat but managed to catch a wing strut and stay with the plane until it crashed into the Chesapeake. Interviewed by Glenn Curtiss soon thereafter, Towers recounted the circumstances of the tragedy; his report and resultant recommendations eventually led to the design and adoption of safety belts and harnesses for pilots and their passengers.

Meanwhile, across the Atlantic and prompted by foresight and good business sense, Britain's Lord Northcliffe threw down his gauntlet by proposing aviation prizes. Northcliffe was Britain's equivalent of America's William Randolph Hearst. He possessed a taste for all things aeronautical, and a keen understanding of the potential of the "aeroplane". With a vast range of publications, he presented his challenge in his London newspaper the *Daily Mail.* In 1906 the paper offered £1,000 ($5,000) for the first flight across the English Channel and £10,000 for the first flight from London to Manchester. *Punch* magazine thought the idea preposterous and offered £10,000 for the first flight to Mars, but by 1910, both the *Mail*'s prizes had been won! On April 1, 1913, Northcliffe came in again offering a prize of £10,000 ($50,000) to the first aviator who successfully crossed the Atlantic in a heavier than air flying machine. Following the *Daily Mail's* sensational announcement, French and Italian aviators were quick to enter the contest while American Rodman Wanamaker, heir to the Philadelphia mercantile fortune, contracted Glenn H. Curtiss to build him a large flying boat.

In October 1913, Glenn Curtiss was visiting England on business and in particular to George Volk's seaplane base on the Brighton sea front. While there, he met for the first time a British aviator and designer, John Cyril Porte. Porte had been interested in aviation from an early age and after he had been invalided out of the Royal Navy submarine service due to the onset of tuberculosis, he flew Deperdussin aircraft in the Military Aeroplane Trials at Larkhill, and in air races at Hendon Aerodrome. Following the collapse and liquidation of Deperdussin from about August 1913, Porte was employed by White & Thompson, a British flying boat manufacturing company as a designer and test pilot and that is where Curtiss and Porte came together. In January 1914, Porte was engaged in building improved Curtiss flying boats for White & Thompson with a flying school attached to the factory, which financially supported the enterprise.

On January 20, 1914, Lt. Towers led 9 officers and 23 enlisted men, with 7 aircraft, portable hangars and other gear from the aviation unit at Annapolis to Pensacola, Florida to set up the first naval aviation training unit. Then on April 20, 1914, Towers led the first naval aviation unit called into action with the Fleet. He and two other pilots, 12 enlisted men and three aircraft sailed from Pensacola aboard the cruiser *Birmingham* in response to the Tampico Affair—a phase of the Mexican Revolution.

With Towers off the scene, and with Curtiss requiring assistance—and a pilot—he turned to his English friend John Cyril Porte. There must have been some chemistry or rapport between the two, for shortly afterward Porte joined Curtiss in the United States and the two men then worked together on a design at Hammondsport—between February and August 1914—commissioned and funded by Wanamaker for a prototype flying boat with which they intended to cross the North Atlantic Ocean and win the prize. Porte and Curtiss produced the *America* in 1914, a larger flying boat with two engines, designed for the transatlantic crossing.

War cloud events brought all to a standstill. On 3 August 1914, Germany declared war on France and Russia, and the next day the Germans invaded Belgium. That same day the United Kingdom declared war on Germany. The First World War had begun.

With the start of war, Porte returned to service in the Royal Navy, which on seeing the promising design subsequently purchased several models of the *America* from Curtiss, now called the H-4. Porte licensed and further developed the designs, constructing a range of *Felixstowe* long-range patrol aircraft, and from his experience passed back improvements to the hull to Curtiss. The later British designs were sold to the U.S. forces, or built by Curtiss as the F5L. The Curtiss factory also built a total of 68 "Large *Americas*" which evolved into the H-12, the only American designed and American built aircraft that saw combat in the First World War.

Meanwhile the *Daily Mail* declared the £10,000 prize to be suspended, and it was not resurrected until 1918, by which time different conditions had been introduced which demanded a "non-stop" flight. Wanamaker was therefore disappointed of his aviation feat due to the war, but the concurrent design improvements from both British and Americans rapidly matured during the war spurring the explosive post-war growth of the flying boat era of International Commercial Aviation, giving Wanamaker at least some claim to being a founding father of an entirely new industry, and the modern world with its characteristically shortened international travel times. Through the American Trans-Oceanic Company he also funded efforts to increase aircraft range throughout the next decade so that Wanamaker's entry, the Fokker trimotor *America*, belatedly flown by Commander Richard E. Byrd transited across the Atlantic only a few days after Lindbergh's historic solo crossing on May 21–22, 1927, winning a new cash prize in the contest. In both cases, aviation and arguably the world, benefited from the sponsorship of Wanamaker.

As 1916 approached, it was feared that the United States would be drawn into the conflict. The Army's Aviation Section, U.S. Signal Corps ordered the development of a simple, easy-to-fly-and-maintain two-seat trainer. Curtiss created the JN-4 "Jenny" for the Army, and the N-9 seaplane version for the Navy. It is one of the most famous products of the Curtiss Company, and thousands were sold to the militaries of the United States, Canada and Britain. Civilian and military aircraft demand boomed, and the company grew to employ 18,000 workers in Buffalo and 3,000 workers in Hammondsport.

When the United States eventually entered the war in 1917, the strength of the country's air power was a sad commentary on the Government's interest in supporting a strong aviation arm. The U.S. Navy's wing consisted of 48 officers, 239 enlisted airmen, 54 airplanes—hardly worthy to be called flyable—and one airship. The idea that airpower could turn the tide in a land war was remote to the Bureau of Ordnance, but Navy pilots had made a good show with a record of 22,000 flights; most of which were flown as reconnaissance and anti-submarine patrols, a few bombing missions and fewer plane-to-plane aerial clashes.

In 1917, the United States was fully engaged in the European War, and concerned about anti-submarine warfare. As a solution, the Navy decided to build flying boats large enough to cross the Atlantic under their own power. Once on friendly European bases, the planes would have sufficient range to hunt and destroy the prowling German submarines. No such airplane existed at the time, so a crack team of Navy engineers led by Lt-Cdr Jerome Hunsaker and Lt-Cdr G. Conrad Westervelt undertook design studies. Glenn H. Curtiss was enlisted as consultant to work out the design's details.

The NC Program

In January 1918, the Navy gave Curtiss a contract for four flying boats after having chosen the trimotor model. The components of the aircraft were manufactured by subcontractors and assembled at the Curtiss plant at Garden City, Long Island. The major components were trucked to the Naval Air Station at nearby Rockaway for final assembly and flight testing. Within nine months of the letting of the contract, the *NC-1* stood assembled at Rockaway. On October 4, 1918, with Commander Holden C. Richardson at the controls and Lieutenant David McCulloch as co-pilot, the *NC-1* rose from the waters of Jamaica Bay for her maiden flight.

For the flying boat's official military designation, Curtiss suggested TH-1 (for Taylor and Hunsaker) as the model's designation. This label was turned down as was Curtiss' second suggestion: DWT for David W. Taylor. The Navy settled on the NC, to identify the Navy–Curtiss collaboration. Curtiss signed the contract to build four NCs in his Buffalo plant at a cost of $125,000 per unit. These were identified as the *NC-1* through the *NC-4* as a numerical sequence within the Naval ship numbering methodology.

Curiously, the Navy thought of the NCs as ships rather than aircraft—perhaps because of their ability to float and "sail" on water. Later however, those familiar with the planes referred to them by the droll nickname "Nancy Boats" in a logical voicing of their letter designation.

With peace declared in Europe on November 11, 1918 the need for these huge, expensive flying boats had passed. However, on the preceding October 31, Commander John H. Towers advised the Chief of Naval Operations that the NCs would be able to fly the Atlantic before the summer of 1919. Several routes were studied and it was determined that the NCs did not have the range to fly non-stop from Newfoundland to Ireland or England. The flight would therefore have to be made by way of the Azores and Portugal. On February 4, 1919, Navy Secretary Josephus Daniels approved the four planes and their mission.

4

Production

In September 1917, Admiral David W. Taylor, chief of Naval Construction Corps, cut corners with a centralized joint team of experts and proponents dedicated to building and flying the Navy–Curtiss Number 1. He gathered his principal men for a critical meeting and at the table were Commander G. C. Westervelt, Commander Holden C. Richardson and Jerome C. Hunsaker. By the meeting's end, these Naval Constructors understood their task was to build what the combined efforts of England, France and Italy were unable to do—build a flying boat capable of carrying enough explosive ordnance as well of defensive armament sufficient to counteract operations of the German submarine menace.

"It seems to me," said Admiral Taylor, "the submarine menace could be aborted, even if not destroyed from the air." He went on to muse that this could be accomplished by large flying boats, which could carry heavy depth charges and machine guns on long ocean hunts. This approach was conceived to conserve valuable shipping space for armaments on Navy transport ships. These flying boats should be able "to fly the broad Atlantic under their own power." With these words, the Admiral indicated to Hunsaker and Westervelt that he was committing the Navy, as a matter of logic, to performing what had previously been considered a fool's errand. Taylor's two junior officers received their order to make the plan a reality; they agreed immediately on the first step—they contacted Glenn Curtiss inviting him to talk with them in Washington.

By summer of 1917, the United States was fully engaged in the brutal European war, and Glenn Curtiss was fully engaged building airplanes for the Navy; Curtiss's friend John H. Towers, now a lieutenant commander was on duty in Washington.

Curtiss was not merely another manufacturer; he was a knowledgeable aviator–industrialist who had the capital, equipment and manpower to turn sketchy ideas into hard reality. A champion motorcycle racer, Curtiss set the world record of 137 miles per hour; he had a need for speed. Curtiss saw the airplane as a means for even greater speed. Reticent in appearance, he flew like a whirlwind in planes with saucy names such as the *June Bug*, the *Red Wing*, and the *Silver Dart*. He flew faster and higher than any of his fellow aviators in America or Europe and won prestigious trophies by the score. His rich imagination kept dreaming up new airplanes and uses for them, which his capitalist sense turned into working production models. By 1914, he had created and incorporated the Curtiss Motor Company and the Curtiss Aeroplane Company, with a capital value of ten million dollars. Curtiss eventually built more than 200 types of aircraft using sixty-seven Curtiss' patent; what Einstein was to physics, Curtiss was to aeronautics.

Curtiss cheerfully undertook the Navy's challenge presented to him by Hunsaker and Westervelt. He and his engineering staff began work with engineers from the Navy's Bureau of Construction on developing the prototype of an oceangoing super plane—the technological wonder of the twentieth century.

Step by step, during one long session after another, with calculating slide-rules in busy hands and chalkboards white with formulas and equations, the civilian and government teams— prominent Navy scientists, eminent physics professors, Curtiss' distinguished production men and experienced aviators worked out the construction, propulsion and configuration problems of the fantastic new flying machine.

For this new challenge, Commander Richardson was told to design a hull that would be independently seaworthy as light in weight as possible yet maintaining the integrity to survive constant slamming into waves when landing at sea loaded to the gills with twelve-tons of fuel and arms.[1] Richardson's first and most successful idea was a V-shaped hull bottom forty-feet long and ten-feet abeam. The initial design team—Westervelt, Richardson and Hunsaker—protected the tail surfaces against the pounding of large ocean waves by mounting them on hollow wood spars high above the water. As the craft's sketch began taking shape on paper, it began looking very curious, like a wing and tail assembly married to a hull, but not fully committed to it. One might assess the appearance as that of a gargantuan dragonfly pouncing on a fish.

The NC flying boats were originally designed with three tractor engines. This proved to be less efficient than an arrangement with one pusher and three tractor engines. Further calculations of the weight-to-horsepower ratio proved that a fourth engine would lift two pounds for every one pound added by its own weight; the *NC-1* was built as a trimotor and *NC-2* was modified with four engines in tandem pairs. Therefore, it was agreed the re-imagined power plant to be four engines: one on each wing and two in tandem on the centerline. The *NC-3* and the *NC-4* were subsequently built in this configuration. The craft could fly with a total weight of 28,000 pounds; six of those fourteen tons including 1,800 gallons of fuel in its nine aluminum tanks, spare parts, oil, radio equipment and the six-man crew.

American manufacturers appropriate for the task were contracted to build various parts of the plane—hulls, wings, fuel tanks and engines—all of which, upon completion were shipped to the Curtiss assembly plant in Garden City, Long Island. Nearby, at the Naval Air Station, Rockaway Beach, a huge hanger was built, large enough to accommodate two NC flying boats. Also at Rockaway, a special marine railway was constructed to facilitate launching and beaching the planes.

Among the several contractors was the Locke Body Company of New York City. Locke contracted building the wing and tail framework. Certainly, a formidable task because there were 68 fragile panels of varies sizes, some at 12-feet wide by 40-feet long. Transporting the panels through 23-miles of busy New York City streets to the Curtiss assembly facility proved to be a problem that needed creative thought and inventiveness. Young Lieutenant Wetherill applied himself to the tricky transport task. He hired horse-drawn theatrical scenery-moving wagons traversing the streets in the late evening hours thereby avoiding inevitable traffic snarls.

On the violent stormy night of March 27, the *NC-1* dragged her anchor and for three days her bottom was battered against the stony-beach. Her hull was damaged and her lower left wing shattered; also shattered were all hope of flying a four-plane squadron to Europe. Executive decision was made to sacrifice the *NC-2* for repairs to the *NC-1*, saving the remains of *NC-2* for further use as spare parts, if needed. Five weeks later, on the evening of May 5, a fire caused by a spark while fueling was in progress in the hanger at Rockaway destroyed the left wing of the *NC-1*—once again the *NC-2* was sacrificed—giving up her left wing assembly for installation on the *NC-1*.

While *NC-1* repairs were underway, it was discovered that the pilot's dual control column had torn loose and the critical wing and tail surfaces were flapping freely. At the same time that these problems were being resolved, Commander Richardson had concerns. After reviewing results of the towing tank tests, he now calculated that the *NC-1* would be unable to get off the water with a full load of fuel to reach the Azores. Subsequently, the *NC-1* was converted to the same four engine

The *NC-1* at Rockaway Beach with its original three-engine configuration; the navigator Lieutenant Commander Patrick N. L. Bellinger is standing in the nose cockpit at left are the pilot and copilot in the main hull center. *[USN]*

The Curtiss *NC-1* now configured with the four-engine arrangement. *[USN]*

In this archive photograph from U.S. Navy Air Service are the crews of the three NCs before their "hop off" to Trepassey Bay, Newfoundland; *left to right:* Lieutenant Commander Albert C. Read, commanding the *NC-4*; Lieutenant E. F. Stone of the U.S. Coast Guard; Lieutenant Walter Hinton, pilot; Special Machinist's Mate E. Harry Howard; Ensign Herbert Charles Rodd, radioman; Lieutenant James L. Breese; Commander John H. Towers, commander in chief of the squadron, *NC-3*; Commander Holden C. Richardson; Lieutenant David H. McCullough; Lieutenant Commander Robert A. Lavender; Boatswain Lloyd Ray Moore; Lieutenant Braxton Rhodes; Lieutenant Commander Patrick M. L. Bellinger; commander of the *NC-1*; Lieutenant Commander Marc A. Mitscher; Lieutenant Louis Theodore Darin; Lieutenant Harry Sadenwater; Chief Machinist's Mate Clarence Irvin Kesseler, and Machinist Rasmus Christensen.

configuration as the *NC-3* and *NC-4*. By July 1918, reconstruction of the *NC-1* was on schedule for delivery to Rockaway. The *NC-1* was delivered to Rockaway in September, and on October 4 she was ready for her maiden flight; the test pilot was Commander Richardson.

Richardson and his copilot climbed into the cockpit through a hole in the bottom of the center engine nacelle. The cockpit was situated between the wings behind the middle engine; on the bottom of the snug compartment of the hull where crew members and the main fuel tanks were housed, on the side was the outboard engine, and on top by the upper wing in its open station originally designated for a machine gunner.

5

First Flights

Within the Navy interest prevailed in accomplishing the transatlantic flight. Early in July, 1918, Lieutenant Richard E. Byrd, a naval engineer at Pensacola engaged in the study of crashes wrote to his superiors in Washington requesting a transfer and be detailed to make a transatlantic flight in an NC-type flying boat when the boat was finished and ready. Two weeks later, with his request endorsed by his commanding officer, Byrd was in Washington where, with mixed emotions, he accepted orders sending him to Nova Scotia as Commander of U.S. Naval Air Forces in Canada. Byrd's task on the coast of Newfoundland was to seek a suitable rest and refueling station for handling and maintenance of large seaplanes. Assisted by his close friend Lt. Walter Hinton, Byrd spent as much time as possible on navigational problems associated with flying across the unpredictable Atlantic.

Meanwhile, at Rockaway, the first flight was coming nearer. Breathlessly, on October 4, 1918, spectators made up of curious citizens, Government officials, Navy mechanics and technicians watched and waited as the first of these aircraft, the *NC-1*, made its first test flight with the early three-engine configuration. The 36 cylinders roared to life; the carriage eased down the inclined railway into the water and the *NC-1* floated free. Richardson taxied back and forth getting a feel for the controls, eventually he swung into the wind and moments later, to a rousing spectator cheer, the world's largest flying machine rose into the air and into aviation history. Over the period of one year from the start of the program, the Navy–Curtiss team could claim success—the Nancy flew! Richardson's fears were allayed; he had a mild case of anxiety, but the first flight justified his design. On November 25, it flew again, with a world record 51 people on board.

Armistice Day, November 11, 1918, signaling the end of the war in Europe, came before testing of the first NC and construction of the other three of the Navy's initial order had been completed. There was now no need for a long-range anti-submarine aircraft; but happily the Navy's interest in developing a big long-range fighting plane continued.

On the morning of April 21, 1919, Towers and the transatlantic group moved to Rockaway. There, at a conference with the captains of the ocean station ships he gave the start date as May 5.

The commissioning of Seaplane Division One took place on May 3, 1919, in the first ceremony of its kind; giving Towers the status equivalent to that of a commander of a division of ships. *[USN]*

In an exceptional ceremony on May 3, the three NC flying boats were placed in regular Navy commission, just as if they were ships of the line. John Towers formally assumed command of NC Seaplane Division One. His orders signed by acting Secretary of the Navy Franklin Delano Roosevelt, gave Towers a status roughly equivalent to that of a commanding officer of a destroyer task force. Towers chose the *NC-3* as his flagship and then made the crew assignments. Richardson was appointed chief pilot of the *NC-3*; Patrick N. L. Bellinger was detailed to the *NC-1*, and Albert C. Read was in command of the *NC-4*. Walter Hinton assumed the position of co-pilot of the *NC-4*. Marc Mitscher was designated pilot of the *NC-1*. Lieutenant Commander Richard E. Byrd was ordered to go aboard the *NC-3* with Towers, but only as far as Newfoundland.

In spite of the commissioning festivities at Rockaway, and the flotilla of destroyers serving as station ships at 50-mile intervals across the Atlantic, the Nancys were not yet ready, for unforeseeable bad luck plagued Seaplane Division One.

The *NC-4* had not been completed until April 30, and when launched into the bay, took on 800 lb of sea water through leaks. Additional mishaps slowed the ability of the *NC-4* to take off: she slipped on her beaching carriage and sustained damage to her hull and wing support struts. Read's shakedown flight turned into a series of breakdowns. While taxiing in from her first shakedown flight, the control cables to the tail assembly were carried away—a devastating tragedy would have occurred if it happened during a flight.

The *NC-3* was in good flyable condition, but there was still work needed on *NC-1* and the *NC-4*. Navy and Curtiss personnel worked feverishly around the clock endeavoring to get the Nancys ship-shape and flyable. Late on the night of May 4 work on the *NC-1* and *NC-4* was finished, the planes were in the hanger and weary Curtiss men went home. The Navy crew began the fueling operation; it was a time-consuming process, each craft having nine 200-gallon tanks. The fueling

Curtiss and Navy engineers and technicians swarm all over the *NC-4* inspecting for faults and making adjustments when necessary. *[USN]*

A Curtiss mechanic is checking the unique tail section of the Navy Curtiss *NC-4*.

In this *c.* 1918 photo, the *NC-4* on its launching platform appears to be lacking its fourth motor, the so-called pusher, and the three motors already in place are missing their propellers. *[USN]*

The Navy had two more sets of NCs constructed for a total of ten built by the Curtiss Aeroplane and Motor Company, numbering *NC-5* through *NC-10*. The NC construction program ended in 1921. *[USN]*

operation was a very dangerous operation involving primitive electric pumps. At 2:15 a.m. Towers was awoken by excited shouting. The NC hanger was blazing; yellow-orange flames and toxic fumes filled the air emitting from varnished fabric, paint, wood, gasoline and oil feeding roaring flames. Twenty frantic Navy men managed to extinguish the fire. When it was over and damage appraised, portions of the tail of the *NC-4* and one entire wing of the *NC-1* were gone.

The carefully stored spare parts saved from the dismantled *NC-2* including a good wing and tail section were installed on the fire ravaged NC-*1* and *NC-4*. The following day, upon routine inspection, serious cracks were discovered in the *NC-1* and *NC-3* propellers; the balance of the day was spent repairing them. Within two days one bad engine was replaced and the other repaired, but once again the elements were against them; a "Yankee-Clipper" gale set in, a 40-knot nor'easter held the NCs in Chatham for the duration of the storm. Read was frustrated, however during this idle period he received some encouragement from the northern weather dispatcher. Conditions on the Newfoundland–Azores route were so bad that the *NC-1* and the *NC-3* were not going anywhere soon.

On the tranquil Thursday morning of May 8,[1] the *NC-1, NC-3* and the *NC-4* eventually took off from Chatham for Nova Scotia on the first leg of the transatlantic journey. The flight was under the control of Commander John Towers, who was also commanding officer and navigator of the *NC-3*. Offshore of Cape Cod, the center engine of the *NC-4* failed. She was forced to land at sea and taxi to the Naval Air Station at Chatham, Massachusetts for repairs. When the *NC-4* had been lost to sight and her distress call intercepted, Towers had already assumed Read would either land by the USS *McDermot* (DD262) for repairs or return to Chatham. The air was still unstable and turning uncomfortably cold. The planes following the line of station ships passing Placentia Bay and at 3,000 feet the men spotted their first icebergs.

The *NC-3* and the *NC-1* arrived at Halifax without the drama of a serious engine failure. Upon their arrival in the Canadian port, Towers was distressed to learn of the apparent loss of the *NC-4*. Cheerfully, the following morning news of the *NC-4's* safety came as a relief. Towers and his crew had minor damage to attend to, the *NC-3* had cracked propellers but with the help of Lieutenant Commander Byrd new propellers were installed, and on May 10, they were off again. During the eventual flight north, both planes flew through cruel squalls receiving violent buffetings from hot and cold air rushing over the headlands toward the sea. The strain of keeping the big machines on course took its toll on the dual pilots. The final three hours were particularly severe, but upon arriving over Halifax, they were rewarded with a clear bright sky, a calm sea, cheering crowds and screaming factory whistles as the NCs taxied to their moorings.

The *NC-4*, still at Chatham, was being readied for another try on May 13 when the forecast indicated an early departure the following morning was possible. Then another stroke of bad luck; the starter on one of the engines failed to spark. Unfortunately, there were no spares on Cape Cod; Read placed an urgent call to Rockaway and within an hour a New York seaplane was dispatched to Montauk to pick up the needed part. The plan was to send the plane making the pickup at Montauk and then continuing on to Cape Cod. Chatham received a call confirming that the Rockaway plane had arrived at Montauk and was preparing to continue on to the Cape. Although darkness had fallen, Read told the dispatcher to radio them to proceed. Under a bright midnight moon the seaplane arrived and immediately the new starter was installed.

The NC-4 remained in Chatham while the other two were in the air flying to Halifax. Finally, *NC-4* became airborne arriving at Halifax before the other two could start to the Azores.

Fortunately, the flight to Trepassey was swift; a favoring tail wind hurried the *NC-4* along. Read had an unexpected surprise as the *NC-4* came into sight, of Newfoundland's Trepassey Bay; his blood ran cold as he witnessed, there in the Bay, the *NC-1* and the *NC-3* maneuvering as if for takeoff.

As it turned out, his fear of being left behind did not last long. True, Tower was attempting to leave for the Azores without the *NC-4*, actually, he had been trying for several hours, but for some reason neither the *NC-3* nor the *NC-1* could get off the water in the crosswind. Read and Jim Breese knew why the two planes could not lift off. The gauges on the fuel tanks were inaccurate and unless the man pumping fuel knew how to interpret the readings on the glass, too much fuel would be taken on.

Towers had indeed received a favorable weather report on the 15th and did decide to go without the *NC-4*. The forecast for May 16 was even better than the 14th

The *NC-3* taxied up and down Trepassey Bay but was unable to become airborne no matter how much she revved her engines because she was overloaded with fuel. *[USN]*

The *NC-4*, still without her fourth motor's propeller is nearing completion. *[USN]*

On her launching-pad the *NC-4* is eased into Jamaica Bay. *[USN]*

In this official United States Navy photograph the *NC-1* is seen landing at Trepassey Bay, Newfoundland, May 1919.

and the commanders of the other two flying boats did not want to leave without the *NC-4*. Now the gaggle of three could all leave together.

With the guarantee of favorable weather, they were back on the water when a piece of rubber was discovered fouling the *NC-4's* fuel line blocking fuel to the thirsty engines. While floating 18-miles from shore the engineers cleaned the carburetors, replaced spark plugs and, just a little after noon the *NC-4* was airborne again.

6

The Flight

Dozens of ships were stationed along the flight path from Newfoundland's Trepassey Bay to the Azores to aid in navigation and rescue if needed. A picket line of 14 ships was assigned from the Azores to Lisbon, and 10 ships from Lisbon to Plymouth.[1] That sort of methodical planning and heavy investment typical of the moon landings 50 years later demonstrated the importance that the Navy placed on it. National prestige was at stake.

The crews donned their leather flying suits over wool uniforms; some choosing an additional layer of protection of wool long-john underwear against the perceived chilling effects of the Atlantic air whistling past the crafts' open cockpits. With the last important piece of gear in place—aviator helmets complete with intercom headsets allowing crews to communicate above the roar of forty-eight cylinders exploding overhead.

Commander Read wrote in his log, "Sun came out, weather is clearing." Then everything went wrong. Once again the *NC-4* seemed unable to shake off its run of bad luck. Shortly after taking off his after-center engine, the pusher, quit; then, while moping along at reduced speed, a second engine coughed-up a connection rod spewing a shower of steam and water and coming to a dead stop. The *NC-4* came fluttering down in a forced landing. At this point, communications were also dead; the long-range transmitter's anemia, a weighted wire, could not be engaged because it was underwater.

Frustrated by the inability to repair the two failed engines, Read ordered pilots Elmer Stone and Walter Hinton to restart the two remaining engines and begin taxiing. Through the long, chilly night the crippled craft slogged along a course plotted by Commander Read. At 5 a.m. Friday May 9 the *NC-4* arrived at Chatham, Cape Cod not as an airplane, but behaving more as a surface vessel.

On May 10, Read thought, somewhat wearily, that he had little chance to complete his mission. Time for the beginning of the transatlantic flight was ticking away and the estimated time for the replacement engines was almost one week. Read reasoned that headquarters might order the *NC-1* and the *NC-3* to leave without waiting for arrival of the *NC-4*. Those two planes flew to Trepassey Bay May 11 landing neatly on choppy water; there waiting for clear skies and orders.

The *NC-4* is beached—judging by the background, the location is probably Rockaway. *[USN]*

Finally, under a clear cloudless sky the *NC-1* and the *NC-3* flew northeast covering the 540 miles to Nova Scotia easily gliding down to a watery landing and a cheery welcoming by the American Consul to Halifax. Towers' and Bellinger's worry concerning turbulent weather and clear skies was Read's opportunity. On May 14, Read flew off to Halifax.

On the afternoon of May 15, the *NC-4* was continuing on its way to Halifax being pushed at ninety-five miles per hour by choppy turbulent air. Read's crew were clearly aware that the other planes had by now received orders to proceed without them, with the proviso, "if the commander deemed prudent". When coming in, banking low over the narrow harbor, they were relieved to see the long wings of their sister crafts sheltered near the USS *Aroostook* (CM3).[2] The two had attempted take-off earlier, but once again a miscalculation of their gross weight had them overloaded and all the frantic gunning of engines failed to lift them from the water.

At long last, on Friday, May 16, all three planes were ready. Again curious crowds of onlookers gathered on the shore—on fishing trawlers and Navy ships personnel leaned against the rails hoping for a good vantage point.

The three NCs taxied out into the bay, sun-rays reflecting off their bright yellow fabric wings—sparkling. The roar of their gunned engines floated back to the shore crowded with curious citizens. Each plane moving slowly at first, jockeying for its take off position, and then increasing speed throwing up a rooster tail-plume until each 28,000 pound machine rose from the water becoming airborne

It was 6 p.m. in New York; an hour later in Newfoundland, and 10 p.m. by the aviator's clock set to Greenwich Mean Time (GMT) when the three boats taxied out into Trepassey Bay for their take off.

That the *NC-4* had joined the others was partly due to the stubbornness and courage of the *NC-4*'s engineer Lt. Breese. When one engine refused to start, it was Breese who when diagnosing the problem determined a weak battery was the

The *NC-4* makes its splash-landing at Halifax. The U.S. Navy achieved the first transatlantic flight eight years before Charles Lindbergh became world famous for crossing the Atlantic nonstop and alone. The Navy wanted to prove the capability of Yankee technology and the airplane as a transoceanic weapon.

Airborne at last! In this Underwood and Underwood photo postcard the *NC-4* is 60 miles at sea heading for Newfoundland's Trepassey Bay.

cause, he then quickly secured a more powerful standby. With neither time nor wiring available for a proper temporary connection, the always insightful engineer joined the battery to the balky ignition system with his pen knife opening the blades forming a 'U' with the knife handle in his hand. When the pilot engaged the starter, the engine did indeed fire—causing Breese to receive a severe electrical burn.

Once again, the *NC-4* banked and strained forward into the wind with all four engines howling. Under the burden of 1,600 gallons of fuel and oil, each plane rose sluggishly; the *NC-1* barely skimming the water as she cleared the harbor. In the deepening evening, they could see icebergs in the shadowy waters only a few hundred feet below. Soon they reached the first of the guardian Navy ships on its appointed station, then the next as they flew west, deeper into the Atlantic and moonless night.

Looking down through the fading twilight, Read could see the whitecapped ocean dotted with icebergs. As it grew darker, it became difficult to see the other two planes; Read turned on his running lights and a message was sent for the others to do the same—nothing happened. The *NC-1* and the *NC-3* remained obscure in the darkening sky, until each had the foresight to switch on their running lights.

In the starless night, darkness blanketed the ocean and all above it. However, reassuring signals pierced the darkness, the sudden golden-yellow of star shells, the silver threads of searchlights and the flying boats' own green and red running lights blinking in a pulsing rhythm allowed the aviators to keep each other in sight in the black immensity of the Atlantic; each hour moving ninety miles closer to Europe.

Darkness surrounded the lumbering sky boats. Clouds, fog, and turbulent air added to the peril of the flight. Towers' plane was in the lead, but the others could not see him because his tail lights failed to switch on. When the clouds parted, Towers saw the *NC-4* 500-feet below and 100-feet ahead; climbing to avoid her, he glanced up and saw the *NC-3* charging right at him; he could do nothing but hold his breath as it whizzed by him a mere 50-feet above.

The *NC-4* was faster than the others. Read became aware of his plane's speed after leaving Rockaway. It was difficult for him from not overtaking and passing Towers in his flagship. If Read ordered his pilot to slow down the big ship became difficult to handle. Soon he was far ahead and was forced to compensate for his speed by flying a circle, coming up behind the formation.

The three planes were again in sight of each other and the station ships until about half way across the Atlantic. All the planes had a radio for communication among themselves and the ships, however their range was limited. The radio on *NC-1* failed, but use of its airborne radio as a navigational aid was a noteworthy milestone in navigation. Morning came on finding the three flying boats in opaque fog; they lost contact and flew on in blind solitude, each commander relying on his navigator to keep them on course.

The *NC-1* and the *NC-3* soon believed themselves lost. Their radio compass equipment had failed and was not picking up signals from the station destroyers, as they rushed on into a thick milky infinity through which no sun or sea was visible, Towers and Bellinger independently reached the same conclusion; rather than flying off their planned course and run out of fuel—perhaps hundreds of miles from any hope of rescue—they would use their capacity for water landing and sit down until the weather cleared enough for observations and a fix. Bellinger decided to go for a landing on the sea and endeavor to get a position fix relative to the ships with his radio direction finder. Unable to locate the station ships in bad weather, the *NC-1* drifted north on the planned course. Commander Bellinger thought he was on course when he spotted a U.S. Navy ship, mistaking it for one of the station ships he continued on his erroneous path. With his airborne radio of no use, he eventually determined the *NC-1* was lost (by an estimated one hundred miles off course).

After estimating his true position Bellinger planned he would take off in the correct heading. Alas, that was not to be. The sea was rougher than it appeared from the air, and after making a hard landing, the *NC-1* was seriously damaged. With the radio directional finder battery dead, one engine was started in an attempt to charge the RDF battery. The station ship's crews were unable to pick up the *NC-1's* weak distress signal. After a day of drifting, the *NC-1* was rescued by a passing Greek ship, the *Ionia*, which endeavored to tow the sea plane, but the line parted. Two U.S. Navy ships were soon on the scene and took over the towing operation, again the towline broke and the *NC-1* was left to sink. The *Ionia* took the *NC-1* crew to Horta.

Down in the sea only fifty-miles from Ponta Delgada, Towers signaled the USS *Harding*, "Stand off, we're going in under our own power." Commander Towers had been, since 1914, the driving force and guiding genius of the plan to cross the Atlantic in an American airoplane. *[USN]*

The *NC-3* drifted off course to the south, he ran into fog so thick he could not read his control panel board.

Like Bellinger, Towers elected to land at sea with the intension of getting his position through his craft's RDF. Surprisingly, he was only 50-miles south of the western end of the Azores. Although the landing was without mishap, the take-off was upset by rough seas, which took a toll on the machine. Initially, one wing was dislodged from the fuselage causing the loss of a pontoon forcing crewmembers to scramble onto the reaming wing endeavoring to keep the plane balanced. Commander Towers, an astute seaman, ordered removal of the offending wing's fabric thereby reducing the chance of accumulating water pudding and the chance of tipping over of the plane. Towers, calling upon his knowledge as an accomplished Navy seaman, with his intrepid crew sailed their stricken craft 205 miles in two days, floating backwards, into Ponta Delgada Harbor on May 17.

Amusingly, neither plane was far off target. The *NC-1* was about an hour's flight west of the Azores island of Flores, while Towers was a bit to the south. Both crews huddled in the rocking, creaking, disabled boats, listening to radio messages to which they could not reply and struggling to keep their derelict craft from sinking.

This extraordinary statistic remains; the disabled *NC-3* had flown 15 hours and 30 minutes and sailed 205 miles in two days still beating the *NC-4*, by two days, which was weather-bound at Horta.

Juan Terry Trippe

Early in 1919, a young Naval Aviator by the name Juan Terry Trippe, then at Yale, published an article in the *Yale Graphic* regarding the preparations of the NC boats. He predicted that the expedition would "demonstrate that a flight across the Atlantic Ocean is a perfectly safe proposition and not a gigantic gamble." Trippe, the visionary was destined to be the founder, president and chairman of the board of the Pan American World Airways.

Twenty-years to the day that the *NC-4* flew from Horta to Ponta Delgada, Trippe was standing on a pier at Port Washington, New York, on the other side of Long Island from Rockaway. He was watching his *Yankee Clipper* take off on the inaugural flight of a regularly scheduled transatlantic air mail service. The *Yankee Clipper* was a Boeing 314 flying boat, three times the weight of the *NC-4*; just one of her Wright Cyclone engines had almost as much power as the *NC-4*s four Liberty engines combined. Two days after a stop in Horta, the *Yankee Clipper* was in Lisbon; a month later the *Dixie Clipper*, a sister ship, made the first flight of scheduled passenger service across the Atlantic. It was 20 years between the historic path finding flight of the *NC-4* and regular mail and passenger service. One can wonder who the greatest visionary was in 1919: Juan Trippe, who predicted such a flight, would be "safe and sane," or Lt-Cdr Albert C. Read who wrote, "Anyone in the present age of new and startling inventions who says positively that we will never attain an altitude of 60,000 feet, will never fly at 500 miles an hour or will never be able to cross to Europe in the forenoon and return in the afternoon, is a most courageous person, with a courage similar to that of those doubters in the olden days who proclaimed that iron or steel ships would never be successful."

Trippe and Read were both right.

The five-leg flight began on May 8, 1919, from the Naval Air Station at Rockaway Beach, New York. It followed a route to Nova Scotia, Newfoundland and the Azores archipelago in the middle of the Atlantic; Lisbon, Portugal and Portsmouth, England. Only *NC-4*, commanded by Albert C. Read, flew the whole way. The entire trip took 24 days.

7

Safe Arrival

The *NC-4* was dead-set to beat the British, and the indefinable Read came through. He landed in the Azores at Horta; while he waited to take off for Portugal, the British team crashed 1,100 miles out from Newfoundland. Other teams were about to attempt the flight, but on May 27, the *NC-4* splashed down off Lisbon, 19 days from New York to complete the first crossing the Atlantic by air.

The flight marked the first use in aviation of the radio compass, air-to-ground, air to air and intercom radio systems, the bubble sextant, wind and drift indicator, the Great Circle air route to Europe. When the unflappable Commander Read and his crew of courageous aviators touched down in Lisbon Harbor at twilight on May 27, 1919 they became the first men to cross the Atlantic by air. Four days later the *NC-4* landed at Plymouth, England.

The first hop to Plymouth on May 30 was along another line of station ships most of which Read failed to spot because of the weather. The *NC-4* arrived at Plymouth making a celebratory victory lap flyby before landing at 2:27 p.m. to a riotous welcome. This last leg of the momentous journey was planned for the sentimental remembrance that it was from Plymouth that the first pilgrims sailed to America in 1620.

Once again it appeared the *NC-4* was going to have unsettled weather to battle, however, about noon the rain clouds dissipated and the sun came out along with thousands of spectators appearing along with the sun. The USS Armed Cruiser No. 2 *Rochester's* radio operator was keeping track of the *NC-4*'s approach receiving reports sent by the station ships. As the *NC-4*'s radio signals became stronger the *Rochester* called Royal Air Force Major R. K. Kershaw who led three F2A flying boats into the air as escorts for the American patrol-bomber. Kershaw flew the American flag between the port interplane struts on his F2A and the British Union Jack between the starboard wing struts.

Suddenly at 2:19 p.m. the *NC-4* appeared through the coastal haze, flying at 1,500 feet, the three F2As trailing behind at a lower altitude. The cheering spectators now had the rare opportunity to gain a perspective between the RAF F2A and the USN *NC-4*; the difference in size of the two was obvious— in comparison the Yankee plane was mammoth.

The *NC-4* took off from Newfoundland on May 16, spanning the Atlantic via the Azores in 11 days; here the flying boat is shown moored at the USS *Shawmut* in Lisbon Harbor.

The *NC-4* was not without its problems; eventually Commander Read spotted Corvo, turned eastward and landed in Horta Harbor at Fayal. Later he flew to São Miguel, then to Lisbon Portugal.

The *NC-4* moored to a wharf in Plymouth Harbor is being pounded by wind and surf. The city's barbican can be seen in the left background.

Read and his five crewmen receive congratulatory handshakes from Admiral Charles Pershall Plunkett aboard the USS Armored Cruiser (ACR-2) *Rochester.*

Commander Read left the *NC-4* with a crew of machinist mates from the *Aroostook* for inspection and general maintenance. Read and his five crewmen boarded Admiral Charles Pershall Plunkett's launch whisking the men to the *Rochester* where they received rousing cheers from the ship's sailors and the ship's band playing Sousa's "America Forever." Here they were received by the ship's senior officers for obligatory hand shaking, back slapping and toasting.

Returning to the Admiral's launch they sped back to the *Aroostook* where they happily shed their flying clothes and became reunited with their clean uniforms which were stowed aboard the *Aroostook* before leaving Trepassey.

Rejoining Admiral Plunkett on his launch, Read and his men sped across the harbor to the waterfront jetty of the Barbican then climbing the stone steps of the monument commemorating the *Mayflower's* departure from this shore.[1]

The Yankee flyers were welcomed by Mayor Joseph Peace Brown, who was turned out dressed in his formal attire: a long flowing crimson robe trimmed with ermine, around his neck a great gold chain with jeweled medallion, all topped off by a tricorn cocked hat. The mayor was attended by three mace bearers; the town clerk was more modestly attired in parochial robe and wearing his shoulder-length white wig.

In his prepared welcoming address to the NC flyers, Mayor Brown said:

> Plymouth is always a point of historic interest to Americans. The memorable sailing of the Pilgrim Fathers from this spot, though comparatively unnoticed at the time was an event which has proved to be a point in history of immeasurable interest. Mainly out of that small beginning a mighty people has sprung up and today in most dramatic fashion , their decedents have crossed back to us in a way never dreamed of by our forefathers and equaling in scientific development and daring the greatest imaginings of Jules Verne.
>
> Your flight today brings our two countries together in the warmest fellowship. Gentlemen, I salute you and welcome you to England.

Soon after the welcoming ceremonies concluded, the official company boarded automobiles and motored to Plymouth's Grand Hotel for a tribute luncheon with local dignitaries. The press of adoring citizens refused to let the American airmen leave the premises without another round of handshakes and hearty cheers.

The following day the three NC skippers and their crews joined Admiral Plunkett on a train for the journey to London's Paddington Station. Upon stepping off the rail car, they were heartedly greeted by scores of American solders, sailors and marines who rushed the heroes, mounting them on their shoulders and carrying them through the station onto the street. The scheduled plan called for the entourage to motor to the Royal Aero Club for another reception planned by RAF aviators. The Yankee servicemen refused to allow the automobile's driver to start his vehicle's engine; they pushed the automobile all the way to the Aero Club while serenading the celebrity flyers with patriotic songs and jaunty jingles.

After meeting and greeting fellow aviators at the Aero Club, the party departed

Commander Read is being carried on the shoulders of American soldiers and sailors through the streets of London, outside of the railroad station just moments after arriving from Plymouth. The crowd consisted of joyfully shouting American and British military and civilians.

for the nearby Hendon Airfield where an RAF air show was in progress. The Americans were especially impressed by the display of aeronautical gymnastics flown by Lieutenant Frank B. Courtney in his twin-engine Boulton-Paul Bourges bomber. Interestingly, eight years later Lieutenant Courtney, who demonstrated so ably the bombers' capabilities, attempted a transatlantic flight, but failed in the effort.

Later in London, Read was pleased to shake the hand of British flyer Harry Hawker. Hawker and his copilot were forced to ditch in mid-Atlantic. Luckily, they managed to put down near a passing ship and were rescued.

After an exciting two-day stay in London, the NC airmen boarded a boat train connection to Paris. Upon arrival in Paris, the Yankee aviators were met by Admiral William S. Benson, Chief of Naval Operations who escorted them to the French Ministry of Marine. Along the way to the ministry building, many citizens lining the therefore recognized Commander Read by his small stature whereas Towers and Bellinger were tall, rough-looking American naval officers.

Soon, from the Marine ministry, Admiral Benson transported the NC crews to the estate where President Wilson was negotiating a peace treaty with the Germans.

Wilson greeting the transatlantic flyers in his usually inelegant way, telling them:

> The entire American nation is proud of your achievement. I am glad to see you and to shake your hand, and I am glad to give you my warmest congratulations. I am happy to be able to say personally how proud I am of all of you. The whole of America and the Navy is most proud of your achievement. I am also pleased that you were able to keep your heads on land as well as on the sea.

Precisely what that last sentence is intended to mean can only be left to speculation. Admiral Benson hurried the aviators from Woodrow Wilson's starched presence to introduce them to David Lloyd George, Georges Clémenceau and Vittorio Emanuele Orlando, the prime ministers of England, France and Italy who added their congratulations. It was a quick tour, and by noontime Towers, Read, Bellinger, and their men were back aboard a train speeding across Picardy for the channel ferry and England, where they had an appointment the next day with the British Air Ministry.

Richard K. Smith, 1973

The Nancy Boat commanders and crews continued their whirlwind rounds of luncheons, exchanging greetings with high-ranking British Air Ministry officials, and meeting such dignitaries as former First Lord of the Admiralty, Winston S. Churchill and heir to the British throne the Prince of Wales.

Aircraft industry delegates were very pleased to meet and talk shop with the Americans. At the June 5 luncheon, some of the well-regarded representatives included Oswald Short, Frederick Handley Page, Sir Thomas Octave Murdoch Sopwith and Colonel John Cyril Porte.

As luck would have it, Commander John Towers and Colonel John Port were—for a short time in 1914—good friends, they were associated with Glenn Curtiss in Curtiss' transatlantic flying boat project. Porte was a naval aviator, who was drafted into the new Royal Air Force. In their conversations, Porte related to Towers his discontent with the Air Ministry's pinch-penny attitude when new or novel concepts were presented. He was particularly upset because of the Ministry's refusal to fund his Porte/Felixstowe *Fury* flying boat, a huge triplane powered by five 334 horsepower engines capable of taking off with a combined fuel, crew and cargo weight of 33,000 pounds.

The following day the American flyers were guests of a group of American expatriates living in London, who fashioned themselves as the American Luncheon Club—meeting weekly for the sport of ingesting fine food and adult beverages. The club chairman explained to their honored guests their reason for abandoning the States was the 18th Amendment to the Constitution—the Volstead Act (prohibition).

The next scheduled event planned for the NC crews was a visit to the Air Ministry, where Read and Towers were decorated with the Air Force Cross, a medal designated for commissioned Royal Air Force officers; Chief Machinist's Mate Eugene Rhoads was pinned with the Air Force Medal which was intended as a tribute for non-commissioned officers and unrated Royal Air Force men.

When pinning a newly designed ribbon on Rhoads' uniform blouse, General John E. Bernard "Galloper Jack" Seely said King George instructed him to deliver a special message to Rhoads. The King sent regrets for missing the ceremony; adding he was sure the success of the flight was due in a large part to Rhoads' engineering knowledge and industry.

After 10 days leave in Paris, the NC Aeronauts returned home.

. . . . .

When in 1957, Breese was flying to Europe; he was asked by the flight attendant if this was his first ocean hop, "No," he replied, "I flew across once before—35 years ago."

8

Radio Log of the NC-4

On May 17, the *NC-4* arrived in Horta on Faial Island in the Azores archipelago—Portuguese Islands in the middle of the Atlantic Ocean. On May 20 the *NC-4* took off for Lisbon but was forced to land, after only 50 miles flown, at Ponta Delgada in São Miguel Island because of mechanical problems. On May 27, the flying boat took off again for Lisbon. After a flight of 9 hours and 43 minutes the *NC-4* arrived at its destination, completing the first crossing of the Atlantic by air. The actual flying time from Newfoundland to Lisbon was 26 hours and 40 minutes.

The flight to Plymouth, England commenced on May 30. After only six hours in the air the *NC-4* was forced to land on the Portuguese coast on the Mondego river to fix a leaking fuel tank. That evening the plane made a brief stop at Ferrol in northwest Spain. On May 31, the stalwart *NC-4* with its resolute crew arrived at Plymouth where they were greeted with an exuberant welcome.

Ensign Rodd's flight log relates with gritty detail the trials and troubling events of the flight.

Ensign Herbert C. Rodd's radio log addressed to *NC-4*'s Commander Albert Cushing Read (edited for brevity)

> The radio installation on the *NC-4* was the last to be completed at Rockaway, the finishing touches being applied about 3:30 a.m. of May 6, the day we were called at 4:30 a.m. to make ready for the start. Due to an unfavorable weather report the flight was delayed and consequently I was able to spend most of the day sitting in the plane, selecting vacuum tubes for both the amplifier and continuous wave transmitter, taking bearings on Norfolk during this afternoon's schedule, to make sure the fixed condensers in the radio compass control panels were adjusted to 1500 meters. This had been done with a wave meter but no test had been made with a station.
>
> No flight had been made to test the radio apparatus and it looked as though we would leave without knowing whether things functioned in the air or not. The weather cleared, however, the afternoon of May 7, and about 5 o'clock we were ready to make a test. Just as we were about to slip down the runway the Engineer Officer [Lieutenant Breese] put his foot through the radio propeller breaking both blades. The center tractor

motor had been turning over and this cause the radio generator to run fast enough so as not to be seen. I told the navigator that it would probably take fifteen minutes to change so we left without effecting repairs as it was growing dark.

I had an opportunity to test the continuous wave transmitter with Rockaway Station and it worked quite satisfactory. The skid fin antenna was used and the buzzer signals were very readable in the air, although the telephone did not work entirely satisfactory except on the water when the motors were stopped. I let out the antenna several times and reeled it in just to see how a metal reel worked, because I had never used one. I was surprised at the ease of operation, especially as there was a sharp turn in the wire.

It appears at this point in Rodd's extensive log dated June 30, 1919, that all his communication systems are in "go" operation. In the next two paragraphs of his report to Commander Read, he expresses joy at receiving messages of congratulation and a welcoming message from the British Air Ministry.

After adjusting the vinometer my radiation showed three amperes on the skid fin antenna, and the *NC-1* came back immediately saying my spark was good. Rockaway then sent a good luck message to me signed, Wise, Jones, Parks and all the rest—all men who had worked hard to get us in shape.

At 2:50 came a long message from Rockaway, emanating from the Admiral Knapp in London, telling us that the British Air Ministry had made arrangements to extend every facility and convenience to NC flying boats at Plymouth after Trans-Atlantic [*sic*] flight and offering us the air station in the Isles of Scilly as a temporary refueling and repair point.[1]

In his log, Rodd writes the three NCs left Rockaway on May 8, heading for Chatham on the way checking communication systems with destroyers on station seriously failing even when only one mile distant. Before reaching Chatham, engines quit forcing a landing at sea.

At 5 o'clock [GMT], 1 p.m. New York time I got the time tick from Arlington, switching it to the Navigator's phones, so he could check his chronometers.

Immediately afterward Chatham Air Station sent a request of our position, followed by a relay from the *Baltimore* at Halifax, giving weather conditions at that point.[2] One thing in the report which alarmed me was a wind velocity of 37 miles per hour from the northwest at 4 p.m. This I immediately passed forward to the Navigator, as we had not yet become accustomed to the intercommunicating phones. Chatham evidently had not heard us acknowledge the message from Admiral Knapp and the Acting Secretary [Roosevelt], as he repeated for which I was obliged to gently rebuke him as it was causing undue interference.

At 6 p.m. *NC-3* sent a message to Siasconset [Nantucket, Massachusetts] to the effect that the NC Division had passed Chatham Light at 5:47.

At 6:30 the Navigator had me send a message to flagplane that we were running on three motors.

At 6:45 we landed [at sea] after having shut sown both center motors. I tried to send during the glide, but could not get a spark, consequently could not tell the destroyer that we were landing.

After we landed, the Navigator passed me a message to send, in the event that I could raise one of the stations. It was to the effect that we were in Lat. 42-21, Long. 68-21, and would probably not need assistance.

I called destroyer[s] 1 and 2 and Chatham, but with no results.

While on the water, Bar Harbor and Cape Sable were heard working the other planes, and ships 300 miles at sea were heard working [USS] *New York* and [USS] *Boston.* Until 2 a.m. the destroyers kept up an almost continuous run of conversation inquiring whether anyone had seen *NC-4* and telling each other which course they were patrolling.

At 5 a.m. we sighted a ship and signaled it with the Aldis lamp, but received no answer. At one time we were within sight of a destroyer, and I signaled long and loud at him but he could not have been listening on shortwave length. Siasconset's signals seemed very loud and I hailed him continuously between 6 and 7 a.m., then called Chatham Air Station. We were off Nanset Light at 6:20. At 9:10 were off the entrance of the channel at Chatham and just at this time I heard Chatham Station tell the destroyers that we had been sighted by Coast Guard Station No. 40.

A boat came out to meet us and we reached the dock at Chatham at 11:35 GMT, 7:35 a.m. Local time.

Shortly after departing Chatham the hard luck *NC-4* returned to fix a faulty propeller; a surprise message from Assistant Navy Secretary Roosevelt lifted the spirits of the *NC-4* crew.

We left Chatham at 12:10 on May 14, but landed at 12:18 to inspect propellers and check an oil line. I worked Chatham on the skid fin antenna during this short period in the air.

We got off again at 9:07 local time. At 1:22 [the] *Boston* was broadcasting on 600 and 952 that we had started flight.

At 2:40 Chatham inquired as to how much gas we had taken and informed us that the C-5 [dirigible] had passed over Chatham at 2:10.

At 8:48 Bar Harbor called and told me to stand by for a rush message from Washington, D.C., to be answered immediately for relaying to all parts of the world. He then sent a long weather report.

At 3:19 the following message was received: “What is your position? All keenly interested in your progress. Good luck, Roosevelt.”

At 3:21 we sent the following: “Roosevelt, Washington, thank you for your good wishes. NC FOUR is 20 miles southwest of Seal Island, making 85 miles per hour, Read.”

Finally, with excellent flying time from Chatham, a successful landing was made at Halifax. The start for Trepassey is then scheduled, but delayed because of another engine problem.

At 5:09 we landed at Halifax. Five minutes previously while in very rough air I worked Bar Harbor, and told him we would land soon. He had requested that I give him a call from Halifax. Operator "DN" Bar Harbor certainly was a good man and it was a pleasure to work fast with him.

The run from Chatham had been accomplished in four hours, so that the storage battery still read high with a hydrometer which we carried, but was charged in the engine room of the [USS] *Baltimore* nevertheless.

The start for Trepassey was made at 12:52 GMT on the following day, May 14, but a landing was made at 1:23 because of no oil pressure on the center tractor motor. I worked the *Baltimore* and *Campertown* Station[s] very well, the distance being 18 miles, according to the Navigator. I told them that we had landed off Stony Head and would leave soon.

The *NC-4* is airborne and heading for Canada; many messages are received and sent; some Station Destroyers complain of not hearing *NC-4's* location; *NC-4* believes other NC planes will start the transatlantic flight without them; another motor change; the *NC-3* goes missing.

We left the water at Stony Head at 3:47 p.m.

At 9 p.m. we passed Destroyer 4, and a few minutes later Destroyer 3 on the Azores leg was heard to tell No. 8 she could not arrive on station until 1 a.m.; that she was taking [the] number 3 position. That was our first suspicion that the other planes were going to attempt a start.

At 9:10 sent a message to Commander Towers requesting that arrangements be made to change forward center motor.

The *Aroostook* told us to look for *NC-1* and *NC-3* as we came in.

A landing was made at Trepassey Bay at 9:39. With the center motor running it was possible to send [messages] during the glide on the skid fin antenna.

The battery was charged aboard the *Aroostook* and a number of spare parts left with Lieutenant Mirick, as everything had functioned well that far and many parts were not considered necessary.

The CQ-1300 transmitter was inspected again and new brushes with stiffer springs put in. The rubber gaskets under the cover had pulled out and rubber tape was substituted. The liner on the propeller tips showed some signs of wear, but went through the flight O.K. The skid fin antenna was taut and there was nothing to do except whip up the apparatus with Three-in-One oil.

The following day at 21:36 GMT (about 6 p.m. our time) we left the water at Trepassey landing again at 21:54 to wait for the *NC-3* and rising again at 22:02.

The *Aroostook* was immediately heard broadcasting the time of our departure and requesting that it be passed down the line to all destroyers.

At 22:50 the *NC-3* was heard testing and communication with her was established at 23:00. She asked if we were just astern of her, to which we asked her to turn on her running lights. We were over station 1 at the time. We passed [station] 2 at 23:35, working Cape Race between ourselves.

NC-1 asked *NC-3* what course he was steering and he replied "150 magnetic." *NC-3* told station 3 to cease firing star shells as they had sighted her. The next set of signals were heard all the way station 10, then over 350 miles distant.

At 02:00 Cape Race asked for a short story of the flight, distance and anything of interest, also asking if I could get a report of the *NC-3*. I was not authorized to do this, so mealy told him that everything was okay.

We passed Destroyer 6 at 02:03 and the SS *Abercorn* asked if she could help in any way. At this point Destroyer 7 was bearing 7-degrees to the right. We passed her at 02:45.

The *NC-1* then inquired whether I had heard the *NC-3*. I listened and found her working Destroyer 13. Shortly after *NC-3* asked Destroyer 16 for a weather report.

Just before we passed Destroyer 14 at 07:06 I heard *Land* [USS *Polar Land*] and *Sierra* [USS AD-18] calling Bar Harbor. Bar Harbor was heard faintly. I sent out our position to Cape Race, but did not hear him answer. The distance at the last time I had worked him was 650 nautical miles. We crossed the steamer lane at this time and there was considerable interference on 600 meters. The SS *Inverton* was working Ponta Delgada. We passed Destroyer 17 at 07:45. [The] *NC-3* was calling [Destroyer] 17 but seemed a good distance ahead according to his signal strength. [The] *NC-1* was loud at this time being just one station behind [us].

At 08:03 the SS *Imperial* wished us good luck and sent his position as Lat. 41-00, Long. 37-00 [steaming from] New York to Spain with gasoline.

At 08:10 NAMG[3] called Cape Race with a message, and at 08:15 NESV told some station that he had met two planes and he had a good time working with them.

At 08:38 the *NC-1* asked Destroyer 6 for a weather report and received a reply in one minute.

At 09:31 Destroyer 17 advised that [the] *NC-3* had just called with a rush message, but that she could barely hear her. This was the last heard of *NC-3* as at 09:45 we struck heavy for aid from then on I stayed up on 1500 meters to get all the compass bearings possible. Although I did not hear number 18 broadcast our passing time, number 19 said we were reported 18 at 09:45.

At 10:30 I asked Destroyer 19 if he had heard our motors, telling him that we were flying between the fog and clouds. She replied that they had not seen us but the operator somehow thought that we were off their port bow. I was just about to ask for compass signals when the Navigator came aft and asked me to inquire about fog close to the water at Destroyers 19 and 20. Number 19 immediately answered that it was very thick near the water and number 20 said it was misty. The wind direction was 83° true at number 19 and 250° [at] number 20. Number 20 inquired if we were flying high or low. I told him, "High but we want to come down if it is clear at surface."

The *NC-3* is off course; the *NC-4* lands at Horta; next stop Ponta Delgada; United States Navy destroyer tender the AD-2 *Melville* delivers a new battery to the *NC-4*, but it is the wrong specific gravity.

At 11:13, I requested weather conditions at Destroyer 21 to which she replied at 11:14, visibility at surface ten miles, wind 200 degrees, [wind] force 20 Miles [per hour].

At 11:31 we sighted Flores and came down near the surface so that I had to reel in the skid fin antenna. I asked Destroyer 22 for compass signals but he did not hear me probably due to a slight change in our time.

At 12:15 I asked Destroyer 23 whether he heard the other planes, to which he replied that *NC-1* passed [destroyer] No. 18 at 10:14 and that he had intercepted a message that *NC-3* was off the course between 17 and 18. He added that he had just heard *NC-1* asking for bearings.

At 13:05 we picked up [the USS] *Land* again, which I told Destroyer 24 I thought was Pico. At 13:14 I started to land and I worked the USS [C-12] *Columbia* as we were coming down.

There was nothing to do to the apparatus at Horta except change the storage battery. The high voltage batteries still read 69 volts, the same voltage as they had at Rockaway. The CQ-130 transmitter was in fine condition, the sparking disc and stationary electrode insulator being only slightly coated with oxide. This was cleaned off with an oily cloth.

[We] left Horta at 12:35 G.M.T. on May 20. The skid fin antenna insulator leaked because we shipped a little water in getting off, so that I could not send until I could let our the trailing wire at 13:00 and sent a broadcast.

[I] Worked the [USS] *Melville* at Ponta Delgada at 13:17. We flew over [station] 24 at 13:22 and two minutes later took a radio compass bearing 351° on Destroyer 25-50 miles [distant].

At 13:37 worked Destroyer 4 [the USS *Wilkes*][4] on the Lisbon Leg and he said our signal was fine as soon as we left Horta.

We passed Station 25 at 13:45. The *Melville* inquired what time we expected to arrive and the Navigator answered, "about 14:20". We were off the harbor about 14:20 and landed at 14:24.

We were not quartered aboard the *Melville*,[5] consequently I could not supervise changing the battery, but sent a message from shore requesting that it be removed from the plane, changed and returned.

The following morning May 21, we went aboard the plane at 5:00 a.m. I found a new battery which when read by hydrometer only showed a specific gravity of 1100. A boat was immediately dispatched for a new one, which read 1250. We did not get off this morning so I was able to get the old battery returned the following day and it showed 1290.

We left Ponta Delgada at 10:17 G.M.T. May 27. For about a half hour I burned the amplifier tubes on 12 volts by mistake and fully expected that I had injured them but upon plugging in 6 volts, destroyers five stations away were heard loudly, so I rested more easily. At 11:09 a message was sent to Admiral Jackson back at Ponta Delgada thanking him for his hospitality and stating that we seemed to be on our way.

The *NC-4* arrives in Lisbon landing in the wrong river and goes aground; causing confusion among station destroyers.

Called the [USS CM-4] *Shawmut* at Lisbon at 17:00, but she did not answer.

We passed No. 11 at 17:05; she had been audible for 25 minutes on the radio compass approximately 40-miles. The [USS CA-124] *Rochester* at Lisbon called us and said that Admiral Plunkett was on board.[6] The admiral then sent a message saying, "Fine work. Come along." At 7:50 I exchanged test communications with No. 4 was carried out. She advised that she had left her station for Ponta Delgada at 14:00. Her signals were still good on 756, but weak on 1500.

I then worked No. 4 again. [The *Wilkes*' radioman] Wiseman said he was only using 4KW and that they would arrive [at] Ponta Delgada about 10 p.m. This indicated that she was about at station 2, [thereby] making the desistance something like 520-miles. I promised him to call him at 18:30 but was busy with the *Rochester* for about a half hour and forgot about the *Wilkes*.

At 19:47, just as the sun was getting low, we entered the Tagus River, landing at Lisbon at 20:01. I sent to the *Rochester* and the *Shawmut* on the skid fin antenna as we were landing.

No reports were necessary at Lisbon. We left there at 05:29 on May 30, circling back over the harbor and finally clearing the main land at 05:55, at which time I let out the trailing wire. The *Shawmut* was busy broadcasting until 6:12, when we sent the following to her: "For American minister. Request you express all heartfelt appreciation of commanding officers and crew of NC-four for wonderful welcome [Commander] Read."

Although originally it was not planned to have destroyers between Lisbon and Cape Finisterre, five were sent out, the *Conner, Rathburne, Woolsey, Yarnall and* [the] *Tarbell*. Using A, B, C, D, and E, respectively for call letters.

At 6:25 [the] CTV *Monsanto* sent the following broadcast: "TransAtlantic seaplane flight now in progress ships are requested to respect use of radio apparatus to avoid interference with the seaplanes. This message did not have much effect, for considerable interference was experienced on this leg from Spanish and Portuguese ships which called each other with QRW signals.

At 07:12 told B [the DD-113 *Rathburne*]: "We may have to land. Stick close on 025 meters for my buzzer modulated set if I send the word 'landing'."

At 07:12 I sent: "We have a gas leak on port motor and may land. [Station] B acknowledged promptly for those messages.

At 07:15 I reeled in my antenna and sent: "Landing, landing, sending on emergency antenna." We landed at 07:21, I had not looked out of the hatch consequently did not know we were landing in a river, else I should have added that information.

At 07:22 the Navigator told me that we were in the Mondego River at Figueira.

At 07:50 we went aground on sand bar and I called B with the battery set. Hearing no reply, I shifted to 756 meters and copied the following, although I missed the call letters: "NC-four passed station A, but *Rathburne* (B) has not sighted yet. Sea smooth."

At 08:30 the *Shawmut* on 756 [meters] sent the following: "To NC-four, what is your situation? Where are you? Answer via destroyer *Shawmut*." Then the following: "Destroyers please listen on 425 meters for message from NC-four."

Then called B, but upon listening found her sending the following to the *Shawmut* at 08:34: "NC-four not sighted, am searching to southward on position. Sea smooth, visibility very good."

At 08:43 the first opening I noticed, I called B again only to hear some destroyer on 756 reply; "Proceeding to assistance of NC-four."

At 08:45 Ensign Dowd, an aircraft radio officer, divining our situation sent the following from *Shawmut*: "Destroyers please listen on 425 meters for messages from NC-four." Destroyer C acknowledged this message, but instead of heading it, the operator called ISW about two minutes, and then sent the *Shawmut's* message, repeating each word, very slowly. His intentions were good but we might have sunk several times during the five minutes he was so doing.

When he had finally finished, B called me at 08:51 and asked: "Have you landed?" I answered very quickly telling our position, but when I was listening, A and C were working. A said: "NC-four last seen full speed." B's signal was audible over 100 feet away.

He then sent the following to the *Shawmut* at 09:04: "NC-four reported leak in gas tank. Would probably land. Am sending to southward of position now. Last signal transmitted by NC-four was on emergency radio set."

This shows that B must have heard me say we were landing.

The *Shawmut* did not get all the above messages the first time and it was 09:15 before they finished communicating.

At 09:18, when things finally quieted down, I called B again on the battery set and he answered, After telling him to listen in the future instead of sending, I sent the following message: "In Mondego River. Must wait high tide at two GMT Seaplane [is] O.K., cannot make Plymouth tonight. Request destroyers keep stations. What is best port to north to land within three hundred miles? Request report situation confram [*sic*] and Plymouth. [Commander] Read."

[Station] B advised that our signals were faint, but readable. The distance at this time was between 20 and 25 miles.

At 09:50 the following was received: "We have forwarded and broadcast your message. [We] will land up in the river in about an hour."

I then went up on deck for a breath of air, telling [station] B I would send him at 10:30.

At 10:30 I talked to him on the radio telephone, and at 10:45 Lieutenant Commander Greer phoned that Commander Symington [the *Rathburne's* Commanding Officer] was on his way in a boat.

Captain Read [*NC-4's* navigator and commanding officer] went ashore. At 13:05, B sent us the following by radiophone: "Best port is Vigo Bay. Will you need gasoline? Please inform *Shawmut* of probable movements (signed) *Shawmut*."

At 13:14 the following was sent from B to C having been semaphored to the *Rathburne* by Captain [Commander] Read: "to confran [*sic*] Brest and London from NC-four, request destroyer of coast division nearest Ferrol Harbor proceed there immediately anchor position where seaplane can secure astern and act as tender for the NC-four. Expect leave Figueira one thirty GMT and stay Ferrol tonight, leaving for Plymouth tomorrow morning at eight weather permitting. Read."

We left the water at Figueira at 13:18. At 13:50 the following was sent to the *Shawmut*: "Left Figueira 1:38 GMT for Ferrol. Require no gas."

At 14:51 Station E sent us the following: "[The] *Tarbell* will arrive [at] Ferrol Bay 4:30 pm."[7] And at 14:35 Station D: "Best place north Mondego River is Ferrol and second Vigo. This had been relayed from VIF and was somewhat delayed."

I asked D at 14:56 if she was in position, to which she replied she was. We passed her at 15:10.

At 16:08, we told the *Tarbell* we would arrive Ferrol at 5 o'clock. The interphone world the nearest to perfection at this time.

Greetings were exchanged with the stations at Oporto and Cape Finisterre at this time. At 16:15 Station One sent the following: "[The] *Harding* will act as mooring ship at Ferrol with anchor in inner harbor on arrival unless you wish me to meet you outside."[8]

At 16:20 we replied, "We do not desire you meet us outside."

At 16:21 No. 1 replied that she would arrive entrance Ferrol at 4:45 GMT.

The operator then added that he had heard us 450 miles.

At 16:28 Station E sent: "Will be outside making big smoke."

At 16:37 the station at Ferrol inquired in Spanish if we were "Hydroplane North Americans," to which I replied that we were.

I reeled in at 16:45 and we splashed down on a landing at 16:47.

The *Harding* came in from sea about 15 minutes later. I did not change the battery at this point, even though it had been used considerably at Figueira.

We left Ferrol at 06:27 the following morning (May 31) climbing rapidly, so that I was working on the trailing wire at 06:33.

The *Harding* was sending our time of departure to Station 2 for relaying to ComFran [Command France], Brest and Admiral Plunkett at Plymouth.

At 06:37 Destroyer 4 was heard to send the message to the *Rochester*.

At 06:45 I requested reports from Nos. 2, 3 and 4.

No. 2 replied at 06:51, No. 3 at 07:04, and No. 4 at 07:11 with full reports. The weather was very good at No. 2, good at No. 3 and fair at No. 4.

No. 5 [*Biddle*] was very loud on his compass schedule but two minutes ahead of time, so I called him and corrected his time.[9] Request compass signals from No. 2 at 07:30. His bearing was 5° to the right. We passed No. 2 at 07:43.

At 07:51 I asked No. 3 for compass signals. He started but broke down, then started again at 07:58, at which time his bearing was 30° to the left and at 08:23 40° to the left. It had begun to get foggy, and the Navigator required further readings.

No. 5 then sent a weather report saying that visibility was 15 miles.

At 08:30, No. 3 was 45° to the right getting fainter and at the same time No. 2 to the left changing at 08:48 to 40° to the left. This proved that we were too far inside for the bearing or No. 3 was a stern bearing.

I phoned this to the Navigator and at 09:01 he said No. 4 was in sight.

I had been informed that there would be a No. 6 destroyer [*Stockton*] near Plymouth but had not heard her. At 09:19, I inquired of No. 5. He wasn't sure but that the No. 4 volunteered the information that she was, although No. 6 did not answer when I called.[10]

At 09:31, I was surprised at the signal intensity of the *Rochester* at Plymouth. She was calling with a message and I told her to "shoot it." as her signal was loud and clear.

The following message was received: "Desirable NC-four land inside the breakwater near *Rochester* then taxi to mooring in Cattewater west of Mount Batten plane will probably led you to mooring, *Aroostook* boat at mooring.

As the *NC-4* takes aim for Plymouth skirting France, Rodd is in constant communication with the station destroyers requesting weather reports. Communications between *NC-4* and station ships are not always the best.

I requested weather reports from the *Rochester* as I told her I couldn't get No. 6. No. 6 evidently heard this because at 09:50 she sent full report saying that visibility was seven miles on surface and hazy overhead. At 09:56 the *Rochester* sent the following: "Weather in Plymouth fine, light northeasterly breeze, clear overhead but slightly hazy around horizon; apparently splendid flying weather. [The] *Stockton* is in position.

I had neglected to get bearing from No. 5 and at 10:01 she was between 45° to 50° to the right. As we had been to the eastward of the line, I assumed that we might have passed her.

At 12:21, No. 6 sent a weather report saying conditions were improving (they were anything but that where we were). And inquiring what time we would arrive at his station, I replied that we had passed No. 5 about 10 a.m. and I thought we were going to fly over Brest.

Then I happened to think about getting a time tick from the Eiffel Tower, but upon inquiring of No. 5, I learned I had just missed his schedule. I learned that Nauen, Germany, sent at noon but at 4000 meters was beyond the range of my receivers.

At 10:50, the *George Washington* at Brest called and informed us that she would handle any messages from ComFran. We were flying low at this time and I was using the skid fin antenna. At 11:10 Brest Station called and said "Bon voyage, bon jour." Not knowing much French, I could only answer, "merci."

Between 11:20 and 11:45 the *George Washington* tried to talk with their powerful radiophones on 1800 meters, but either this modulation was poor or else we were too near, for although the carrier wave was extraordinarily loud and the tune remained study, I could not understand the voice. All I got was the word, "congratulations."

At 11:15 I had sent the following. "To confirm Brest greeting NC-four, I am sorry we cannot stop. [Signed] Read"

To which the following reply was received at 11:43. "To NC-four, congratulations on your magnificent feats. Sorry you cannot stop and let us entertain you. Good Luck. [Signed] Halstead."

Leaving Brest we flew very low and not until we had sighted Plymouth were we high enough at any time to let out the trailing wire. The *George Washington* had difficulty in hearing our signals after we left and communications was maintained through the USS *Hannibal* at anchor at Brest.[11, 12]

At 12:00 and 12:07 No. 6 sent weather information saying visibility was seven miles and the sun was shining. We were flying very low in fog and only using small antenna. She replied that our signals were faint but getting louder.

At 12:25, No. 6 informed us she was making heavy black smoke and that our signals were good.

At 12:30 her bearing was 50° to the right and three minutes later it was 55° to the right (or reciprocal).

I then asked if our signals were louder. Their reply was, "They seem about the same."

At 12:41, No. 6 said that the visibility was eight miles and that our signals were weaker.

At 12:41, I told No. 6 that I thought we had passed to the eastward of her.

At 12:51 upon looking out of the hatch, I saw a merchant vessel. I could not distinguish what flag she was flying but I hoped she could tell us his position and thus we would know ours. I sent the international abbreviation for, "for what ship is this?" and "what's your position?" The operator must have been on deck watching us for no answer was received.

At 12:57, No. 6 sent the following: "There are two sailing vessels about four miles apart, breaking 150° true eight miles from the [DD 73] *Stockton.*

We had not seen them and I had visions of missing Plymouth, so I asked the Navigator if it would be possible to climb to 400 feet so that I could call Plymouth Station and request compass signals. It has always so much easier to take compass bearings on a shore station that I thought I would be able to get accurate bearings and help find the harbor. We started to climb but had to come down again.

The *Rochester* then called at 13:10, and said our signals were getting louder.

Her signals were good but not as good on the skid fin antenna as they were on the trailing wire as they were four hours previously when we were only half way across the Bay of Biscay, consequently it seemed to me Plymouth was much further distant than it really was.

At 13:12, the *Aroostook* called with best wishes.

At 13:15, I was able to put out the trailing wire as we had sighted land and found ourselves headed right for the harbor.

At 13:19, No. 6 called and said the visibility was ten miles and the sky clear. I told her we had sighted land and were all right.

At 13:25, we spiraled down and landed inside the Cattewater at Plymouth, ending the flight.[13]

The U.S. Navy mission designed to challenge and conquer the Atlantic Ocean by air is safely ensconced within the pages of the world's aeronautical record books: a technical success, even though it was not a pretty one. Our fearless Aeronaughts are welcomed as heroes and on the receiving end of countless heroes' receptions.

9

Returning Home

While touring Brest, France, the flyers received their transport orders for returning to the States. On June 15, for their trip to New York, the three NC crews boarded the 12,450-ton USS *Zeppelin*. The *Zeppelin*, a German passenger and freight airship, was turned over the United States Navy after the Armistice.

> She [the *Zeppelin*] was commissioned at Portsmouth, England on March 29, 1919, and her first commanding officer was Commander Theodore G. Ellyson, Navy Aviator No. 1. One thing that Ellyson never expected from his Navy aeronautical career was that he would some day command a German-built Zeppelin, much less the type of Zeppelin he was given.
>
> Richard K. Smith, *First Across,* 1973.

Passengers on this day's flight, besides the NC crews, included U.S. Army officers and men, returning from occupation in the Rhineland; some soldiers with their war brides and young children.

An interesting note for inclusion in this tale is that during the flight home, Commanders Read, Towers and Bellinger and other crewmen gave talks to interested passengers about their experiences during and after the their harrowing transatlantic flight.

Hostile weather plagued the NCs' flights to Europe and it was no less friendly during their flight home. Torrential rain pelted the *Zeppelin* when it swung low at Ambrose Light picking up the pilot while steaming into the narrows between Fort Hamilton and Fort Wadsworth guarding New York Harbor.

Excitement reigned, as the *Zeppelin* moved across the lower bay, many submarine chasers, submarine petrol craft, torpedo boats and Navy tug boats swarmed around escorting the skyship. Flying at a respectable distance overhead of the *Zeppelin*, the Rockaway stationed blimp the *C4* tracked the ship's course as two F-5L flying boats flew circles around the *Zeppelin*. Suddenly, a DeHavilland DH4 from the Mineola Army Airfield charged out of the grey sky diving low over the *Zeppelin* dropping packets containing invitations for the NC heroes to attend a dinner in their honor.

As the skyship is approaching the Battery, the submarine chaser the *Herreshoff* sweeps in close, then a newspaper man, a former Navy signalman, sent a semaphore message to the *Zeppelin* saying the wives of the NC's crews are aboard the *Herreshoff.*

> The tugboat *Manhattan* also met the *Zeppelin* off the Battery, and on board her were such VIPs as Glenn Curtiss, Rear Admiral Bradley A. Fiske, Captain Robert A. Bartlett and Alan R. Hawley of the Aero Club of America, among others. These persons were present at their own initiative; they were not an official delegation. There was no official delegation to greet and fête the NC flyers because that custom which became institutionalized in the 1920s had not yet been invented.
>
> Richard K. Smith, *First Across,* 1973.

The NC crews were allowed to go ashore first; they were welcomed by Third Naval District Commandant Rear Admiral James H. Glennon. After a brief welcoming ceremony, the crowd of admirers swept in surrounding the aviators for handshakes and autographs. Fully an hour passed before they could get away to join their wives and families in a nearby customs office. Also present were newspaper reporters eager to question the men. It is a matter of record that Commander Read, in his succinct manner, answered the reporters who were seeking a statement of the excitement of the transatlantic flight, were disappointed when he told them, "My flight for the most part was quite a monotonous affair; it was simply doing the same things over and over again from start to finish."

John Towers told the news hounds, "The principal lesson learned from the experience of the NC expeditions is the necessity of developing a radio direction finder for transatlantic flights..." Taking a breath, he added, "and establishment of a meteorologist system by which weather in all quarters over the ocean may be reliably reported." Continuing on that thought, he said, "... meteorological stations will be commercially profitable." Such a system did not come on line until January 1940.

Interestingly, Towers did not see a future for transatlantic airplane operations. Rather, he predicted the future held substantial opportunities for dirigible travel. Commandeer Read agreed with Towers' observation—for added weight he interjected, "Crossing the Atlantic by seaplane will not be commercially profitable soon; the dirigible will accomplish more along this line within the next few years."

From Hoboken, the NC flyers, their families and friends ferried over to Manhattan where they met Glenn Curtiss who had prepared a gala celebratory reception in the Commodore Hotel for the distinguished flyers.

An interesting footnote to the celebration is that each attendee received a piece of fabric from the *NC-4's* wing as a souvenir. Occasionally, one of these pieces of souvenir fabric is offered for sale on the Internet auction site, eBay.

10

The Handshakes End

So, that was that!

No ticker-tape parade along Broadway awaited the flyers; the newshounds went on to other more pressing stories. The NC Aeronaughts were yesterday's news; the interest of the fickle citizenry moved on to other subjects of the day. The Senate was unreceptive to President Wilson's negotiations and signing on to the Versailles Treaty; there was racial turmoil in the capital city, there was talk of passing a gun control law, and the District of Columbia was on the brink of bankruptcy.

On June 30, the NC commanders and their crews reported to Secretary of the Navy Josephus Daniels. Daniels extended his warmest congratulation to the men; he made the grand announcement that in appreciation of their superior achievement, the Congress planned to commission a special medal be struck by the mint honoring their transatlantic flight. The medals' face and obverse would be the same on all, except Read's would be gold, Tower's and the *NC-4s* crews' would be silver and all others flyers' medals would be bronze. After the brief ceremony, the flyers, Secretary Daniels and Assistant Secretary Roosevelt posed for an archival photograph on the steps of the State, War and Navy Building.

With their last official "welcoming" obligation fulfilled, the celebrated NC comrades went their separate ways—disappearing back into their private and military careers. Soon they were forgotten and all but fully discounted by a capricious American public.

For a brief moment in time the *NC-4* flight was of paramount interest to Americans; that interest faded as quickly as a sunset over the western ocean. Americans love a hero until another comes along shining brilliantly until his luster also fades, and so on. Nothing proves this as wonderfully as the pinch-penny United States Congress. A decade sped by before Congress got around to appropriating the insignificant funds needed for striking the special NC medals.

Following the 1928 Congressional Gold Medal awarded to Charles Lindbergh for the first solo transatlantic flight, Representative James Russell Leech of Pennsylvania sought to recognize the *NC-4* crew. In 1929, he introduced legislation to honoring the accomplishment of the *NC-4* team, for the first transatlantic flight.

The United States Congress passed Public Law 70-714 on February 9, 1929. This created the legal authorization to award specially minted medals to the members of the *NC-4* crew. The law read:

> Be it enacted by the Senate and House of Representatives of the United States of America in Congress assembled, That the President be, and is hereby, authorized to award, in the name of Congress, gold medals of appropriate design to Commander John H. Towers for conceiving, organizing, and commanding the first trans-Atlantic flight; to Lieutenant Commander Albert C. Read, United States Navy, commanding officer *NC-4*; to Lieutenant Elmer F. Stone, United States Coast Guard, pilot; to former Lieutenant Walter Hinton, United States Navy, pilot; to Lieutenant H. C. Rodd, United States Navy, radio operator; to former Lieutenant J. L. Breese, United States Naval Reserve Force, engineer; and to former Machinist's Mate Eugene Rhodes, United States Navy, engineer, for their extraordinary achievement in making the first successful trans-Atlantic flight, in the United States naval flying boat *NC-4*, in May, 1919.

The Underwood and Underwood photographer captured Lieutenant-Commander Albert Cushing Read in readiness for his long transatlantic journey scheduled to begin on May 16, 1919.

On May 23, 1930, a small contingent of NC flyers journeyed to the White House where President Hoover pinned the decorations, won eleven years earlier, on the men's jackets.

The people of England, Portugal and France are astutely aware of the importance of remembering and honoring events of historical importance, and they have done this for millennia, which is directly opposite of Americans who are blasé about their four-hundred year history.

In 1920, the historically-minded British erected a plaque on the Portsmouth Barbican celebrating the *NC-4*'s arrival; in 1949, the Portuguese placed a similar marker in Lisbon, and in Trepassey, Canada there is a plaque recording the *NC-4*'s brief stop there. In the United States, fifty-years passed before a modest marker became a reality at Rockaway, New York paid for and erected by the citizens of that community.

11

Personnel

The Navy selected crews to man the three NC planes, appointing Towers as commanding officer. Crews came from the regular U.S. Navy, the Naval Reserve and the U.S. Coast Guard. Towers chose *NC-3* as his flagship, and Richardson was picked as chief pilot. Patrick N. L. Bellinger was chosen as commander for *NC-1* and Albert C. Read for *NC-4*. Marc Mitscher, originally picked to command the scrubbed *NC-2*, became *NC-1*'s pilot. In addition, the airplanes carried radio operators, flight engineers and mechanics.

Albert Cushing Read

(March 29, 1887– October 10, 1967)

Read graduated from the United States Naval Academy in 1906 and was commissioned an ensign in 1908. He advanced through the grades to Rear Admiral in 1942. He was detailed to Naval Aviation in 1915 and for a flight across the Atlantic in May 1919 commanding the *NC-4* flying boat in a trip from Rockaway, New York, to Plymouth, England, via the Azores, Portugal and Spain.

During his career, he was awarded the Distinguished Service Medal, the Legion of Merit, and the special gold *NC-4* Medal. The triumph of the first flight across the Atlantic was that of Read's and his crew of fearless aviators. As captain of the first successful transatlantic flight, he was presented the Portuguese award of Commander of the Military Order of the Tower and Sword, and later in Plymouth, he was awarded the British Royal Air Force Cross, Military Order of the British Empire.

While he served with the fleet, he studied everything available on flying. When the Navy opened its premier training school at Pensacola in 1912, he was among the first selected for training. After his solo-flight in 1915 he was designated Naval Aviator No. 24. When he served aboard the USS *Carolina*, the first Navy ship provided with aircraft, he made numerous catapult take-offs as part of his regular flight operations.

Returning to regular Navy aviation duty he successively served in numerous important commands until the Second World War when he became Chief of the

Air Technical Training in Chicago and then commanded the Navy air activities at Norfolk until the end of the war. For this service, he was awarded the Legion of Merit.

John Henry Towers

(January 30, 1885–April 30, 1955)

John Henry Towers was born in Rome, Georgia, on January 30, 1885. A graduate of the Naval Academy Class of 1906, Ensign Towers served onboard the battleships USS *Kentucky* (BB-6) and USS *Michigan* (BB-27) before reporting to the Curtiss Flying School.

On June 20, 1913, while flying as an observer with Ensign William Billingsley over the Chesapeake Bay in a Wright seaplane, Towers nearly became one of naval aviation's first flying casualties. The plane was caught in a sudden downdraft sending it earthward; pilot Ensign Billingsley was thrown from the aircraft and killed (becoming the first naval aviation fatality). Towers was also wrenched from his seat, but managing to catch a wing strut he remained with the plane until it crashed into the Chesapeake. The accident prompted Glenn Curtiss to design the first personnel safety devices in naval aviation; his designs of safety belts and harnesses for pilots and their passengers eventually became standard in all military, commercial and private aircraft. This is a pattern seen throughout the history of aviation where lessons are drawn from accidents and lessons are learned to save others from repeating the same mistakes.

Over the Chesapeake Bay, Towers conducted tests to advance techniques for spotting submerged submarines from the air. He continued these tests into 1913 during fleet operations near Guantanamo Bay, Cuba. In addition, he investigated the potential for Navy aerial reconnaissance, bombing, photography and communications.

Before the United States became actively involved in the First World War, plans were underway to develop and build an aeroplane capable of transatlantic flight. Planning for the mission actually began when Allied shipping was being destroyed by German submarine attacks, but the transatlantic mission could not be accomplished before the war came to an end.

In 1919, then-Commander Towers proposed, planned and led the first crossing of the Atlantic. Between the autumn of 1919 and the late winter of 1922 and 1923, Towers served at sea—as the executive officer of USS *Aroostook* and as the commanding officer of the old destroyer USS *Mugford*, which had been redesignated an aircraft tender. Then, after a tour as executive officer at NAS Pensacola, he spent two and one-half years—from March 1923 to September 1925—as an assistant naval attaché, serving at the American embassies at London, Paris, Rome, the Hague, and Berlin. Returning to the United States in the autumn of 1925, he was assigned to the Bureau of Aeronautics and served as a member of the court of inquiry which investigated the loss of dirigible USS *Shenandoah*. Towers next commanded USS *Langley*, the Navy's first aircraft carrier, from January 1927 to August 1928. He received a commendation for "coolness and courage in the face of danger" when a gasoline line caught fire and burned on board the carrier in December 1927.

Between June 1933 and June 1939, Towers filled a variety of billets ashore and afloat. He completed the senior course at the Naval War College in 1934 and then commanded the Naval Air Station at San Diego; again serving on the staff of ComAirBatFor. He commanded the USS *Saratoga* (CV-3); and became Assistant Chief of the Bureau of Aeronautics. On June 1, 1939, he was named Chief of the Bureau of Aeronautics with the accompanying rank of rear admiral.

As Aeronautics Bureau Chief, Towers organized the Navy's aircraft procurement plans. Under his leadership, the air arm of the Navy grew from 2,000 planes in 1939 to 39,000 in 1942. He also instituted a rigorous pilot-training program and established a trained group of reserve officers for ground support duties. During Towers' tenure, the number of men assigned to naval aviation activities reached a high point of some 750,000.

Before retiring from a distinctive Navy career, his final assignment was chairing the Navy's General Board from March to December 1947; Towers retired on December 1, 1947. During his retirement years, Towers served as President of the Pacific War Memorial, as assistant to the President of Pan American World Airways, and as President of the Flight Safety Council. Admiral Towers died in St. Albans' Hospital, Jamaica, New York, on April 30, 1955, he is buried at Arlington National Cemetery.

Patrick N. L. Bellinger

(October 8, 1885–May 30, 1962)
Courtesy of the Library of Congress and *National Geographic*, August 1961

Pat Bellinger hailed from South Carolina, graduating from the United States Naval Academy in 1907. His first assignments were to battleship and submarine duty during 1911 and 1912 when the Navy was taking its first cautious steps into aviation.

Bellinger took an early interest in aviation and in 1912, he was among the first group of U.S. Navy pilots certified; he has the distinction of being Naval Aviator No. 8. Always an outspoken advocate of naval aviation, he helped it grow from humble beginnings to a mighty offensive force.

In April 1914, he flew during the occupation of Vera Cruz, Mexico, conducting reconnaissance missions off the USS *Mississippi*, becoming the first Navy pilot returning home with enemy bullet holes in his aircraft.

He set an altitude record of 10,000 feet in 1915 and experimented constantly with bombing techniques, catapult takeoffs at sea, and using instruments on night flights. During the First World War, he commanded the Naval Air Station at Hampton Roads, Virginia, and there began preparing for a transatlantic flight. For his roll in the successful *NC-4* flight, he received the Navy Cross. Later he served in many staff and command positions, including tours as assistant naval attaché in Italy and as commander of the aircraft carriers *Langley* and *Ranger*.

By 1940, he had advanced to the rank of Rear Admiral in command of Patrol Wing 2 based in Honolulu. He was the senior air officer present during the Japanese attack

Lieutenant (jg) Patrick M. L. Bellinger is prepared for take off in the 1915 Curtiss AH-3 hydroaeroplane; his mission is to test a new control system.

on Pearl Harbor and he sent out the first radio alert: "Air raid. Pearl Harbor—this is no drill."

In May 1942, he took command of all patrol wings in the Pacific, and in August became Chief of Staff to the Commander In Chief of the US Fleet, Admiral Ernest J. King. In March 1943, he took command of the Atlantic Fleet Air Force, with primary responsibility for anti-submarine patrols throughout the Atlantic. His promotion to Vice Admiral occurred in October 1943.

For his Second World War service, Admiral Bellinger received the Distinguished Service Medal. As one of the NC-4 Aeronaughts, the Portuguese, French and Italian Governments also decorated him.

He retired from active duty in 1947; he died on May 30, 1962 at Clifton Forge, Virginia. He was buried with full military honors in Section 2 of Arlington National Cemetery

Elmer Fowler Stone

(January 22, 1887–May 20, 1936)

Elmer Fowler Stone was born in Lavonia, Livingston County, New York, on January 22, 1887. His family moved to Norfolk, Virginia in 1895 where he attended high school, after graduating, he began working as a stenographer-typist. In 1910, at the age of 23, he qualified as a cadet in the Revenue Cutter Service of the United States after passing the required examinations, scoring higher than all other applicants. His appointment as a cadet in the Revenue Cutter Service School of Instruction came on April 30, 1910. He graduated three years later, on June 7, 1913, and was commissioned as a third lieutenant in the Revenue Cutter Service.

Stone's first assignment put him on board the Revenue Cutter *Onondaga* on June 13, 1913 where he was detailed to study the steam machinery of the vessel. By November 1 of that year, Stone, feeling he had qualified himself to perform the duties of an engineer officer, requested headquarters to assign him to duty as a line officer and on February 14, 1914 headquarters complied with his request and Stone became a line officer of the same vessel.

On October 9, 1914, Stone was transferred to the *Itasca*, on which he served until February 1, 1915, when he was again assigned to the *Onondaga*. While he was serving on the *Onondaga* he took part in the rescue of seven seamen who had been shipwrecked on the lumber-laden schooner the *C.C. Wehrum* off False Cape, Virginia. For the manner in which he handled his life-saving boat crew, Stone received a commendation by the Assistant Secretary of the Treasury Department. In January 1915, the Revenue Cutter Service combined with the Life-Saving Service forming the United States Coast Guard.

Early in 1916, Stone put in his first request to be assigned to duty in connection with aviation; especially aviation having a direct bearing on assistance to vessels in distress and the search for derelict vessels. On March 21, 1916, he was one of two Coast Guard officers assigned to aviation training. On April 1, 1916, he reported to the air station at Pensacola, Florida. On April 10, 1917, after successfully completing the training, he gained the distinction of being Naval Aviator No. 38 on the Navy's roster of naval aviators.

After the United States entered the First World War the Coast Guard was transferred to the Navy Department, Stone served on board the Navy armored cruiser USS *Huntington*. For his service during the war on board the *Huntington* he was awarded the Victory Medal with a Patrol Clasp. He was detached from Naval Air Station Rockaway Beach in May 1918 and assigned to the Navy Department's Bureau of Construction and Repair. The following month, on June 7, 1918, he was promoted to second lieutenant and one month later he was promoted to first lieutenant.

It was while he was a first lieutenant that Stone made history as the pilot of the Navy seaplane *NC-4* during an attempt by the Navy to complete the first transatlantic flight.

On the May 1, 1935, Stone was promoted to the rank of commander. On May 21, 1935, he reported as the commanding officer to the Air Patrol Detachment at San Diego, California. It was here at the Naval Air Station that he met his death the following year.

On May 20, 1936, Commander Stone, while inspecting a new patrol plane, walked over and sat down on a concrete hanger abutment. He fell over with an attack of coronary thrombosis, resulting in his almost instant death. On May 12, 1983, he was re-buried in Arlington National Cemetery and inducted into the United States Naval Aviation Hall of Honor.

Walter T. Hinton

(November 10, 1888–October 28, 1981)

Hinton's was a family of farmers in Van Wert, Ohio. On his Second World War registration card, for middle name he wrote 'none'. In fact in no document—including birth certificate, passport application and grave does a middle name occur so the initial 'T' seems to be a mystery.

One day as a young man, he saw a colorful poster urging young men to "Join the Navy and See the World". Soon after, he joined the United States Navy. He saw action in the 1914 United States occupation of Veracruz, Mexico. Hinton had a great fascination with early aircraft, and soon joined naval aviation.

Hinton achieved fame as the pilot of the Curtiss *NC-4* flying boat; in addition to his daring transatlantic flight, he experienced further aeronautic adventures during the 1920s. One particularly risky adventure included exploring the Arctic by balloon. In this wayward flight from Rockaway, Queens to Moose Factory Island, a community in the Cochrane District of Ontario, Canada. Hinton survived his balloon's crash, becoming lost in the Canadian Arctic in the dead of winter—he was believed dead. After a month-long trek through the winter wilderness, he returned to civilization. In 1922 to 1923, and again in 1924 he accompanied Dr Hamilton Rice on his Brazil expeditions. In 1923 the seaplane he was in crashed and lost his passport among other items.

During all his wandering adventures, Hinton wrote letters home that his family sold to newspapers, which prompted the Navy to start enforcing rarely used censorship rules.

A valuable resource, the Navy sponsored Hinton touring the country as a speaker promoting aviation for the Exchange Clubs in the United States.

During his long retirement, Hinton lived in Pompano Beach, Florida, where he delighted in sharing his memories with local children. One of the happiest events of his later years was being a special guest on a supersonic transatlantic flight of the Concorde, making the trip in less than four hours, which in 1919, had taken Hinton 19 days.

Hinton was President and Founder of the Aviation Institute of U.S.A., Washington D.C. In 1927 and 1928, he published several periodicals on aviation: Periodicals including *Opportunities in Aviation*; *The Wright Whirlwind Motor*; *Pioneers in Aviation*; and *Aviation Progress*.

New Haven Register, Sunday, November 1, 1981
Walter Hinton, aviation pioneer, one of first crew to cross ocean.
Pompano Beach, Fla. (AP) –

Walter Hinton, an aviation pioneer who was a member of a six-man crew that flew a Navy plane across the Atlantic Ocean eight years before Lindbergh, has died at the age of 92.

Hinton, a Broward County resident since the late 1950s, died Wednesday in the Colonial Palms Nursing Home.

Hinton was born on an Ohio farm on Nov. 10, 1888. He took an early interest in the developing field of aviation and went on to become one of its early heroes.

He made the first flight between New York and Rio de Janeiro and piloted an expedition into parts of the unexplored Amazon River Valley.

In an interview last July when he was honored by the Brazilian government for the Amazon flights, Hinton said he had no idea he was making history with his early exploits.

"There weren't many people interested in it in those days," he said. "The majority of them thought it was just a bunch of daredevils. But I'm still very proud of everything."

Hinton, who was a friend of the Wright brothers and Adm. Richard Byrd, was the last surviving member of the six-man crew which flew the *NC-4* from Rockaway, N.Y. to Lisbon, Portugal, in May 1919.

Lindbergh's epic flight in 1927 was solo.

After his pioneering days, Hinton founded a correspondence school for pilots and served on the Civil Aeronautics Board. Eventually he retired in South Florida.

James Lawrence Breese
(July 12, 1885–April 1, 1959)

Little is known about the life of James Breese. He was born in Newport, Rhode Island in 1885 and was a lieutenant in the U.S. Navy by 1919 and selected to be co-pilot of NC-4. During the Second World War he was Commander of the New Mexico Civil Air Patrol. After the death of his first wife he married Florence Wagner, the widow of Beverley Hills Publisher Robert Wagner. James Breese dies at La Jolla, San Diego, 1 April 1959.

At the Rockaway Naval Air Station all was peaceful and serene on Sunday evening, May, 7 after the Curtiss crew had left for their billets. About two dozen Navy personnel including Lieutenant Breese remained making final adjustments to the *NC-4* engines and keeping watch on the fueling operation.

About 2:15 a.m., Chief Machinist Mate Rasmus Christensen working on the starboard radiator of the *NC-1* dismounted the plane to check the fuel level in the drum feeding the *NC-1's* tanks. As he approached the drum there was a sudden and violent explosion and fire. Later investigation determined the fire was caused by a spark emanating from the fuel pump's motor.

Lieutenant Breese, engineering officer aboard the *NC-4* at seeing the flash and hearing Christensen's alarm swiftly scrambling off his plane's hull, and quickly grabbing a fire extinguisher, he trained it on the flames which had already advanced under the *NC-4's* tail section. Breese's swift actions saved the *NC-4* from serious damage and perhaps complete destruction.

On Thursday, May 8, mechanics crowded around the NC flying boats, each checking their plane's oil in their carburetors, as the engines coughed to life the engineers' watched with care their machine's tachometer, oil pressure and temperature gauges. Commander Towers grave the order to takeoff for Halifax.

The *NC-4's* original forward engine was reduced to trash; it was replaced with a new low compression model. Breese was unhappy with the replacement, however it could get the *NC-4* to Trepassey and a new high compression engine could be obtained from the supply of auxiliary parts aboard the CM-3 *Aroostook* (this ship was a minelayer, which served from 1917 until 1931).

The weather report received aboard the *Aroostook* for Friday May16, was for clear cloudless skies. Shortly after 5 p.m. the NC crews assembled and mounted their flying boats. Towers, in his flagship, gave the order to start engines and go for takeoff. At the word the pilots cranked up their engines—all, with the exception of *NC-4*. The *NC-4's* ignition was faulty during engine test, but Breese thought he had fixed the problem.

Herbert Charles Rodd

(September 7, 1894–June 15, 1932)

Little is known about the life of Herbert Rodd. He was born in Cleveland Ohio and after joining the U.S. Navy Reserves he was commissioned ensign and selected to join the transatlantic team. As radioman he assisted in developing the radio compass used on all three of the NCs. In August 1918, before joining the United States Navy Reserves., Rodd served as a radio operator on the Great Lakes. For his action in the *NC-4* transatlantic flight, Rodd was awarded the Navy Cross.

By 1932 Rodd was still in the Navy and had risen to the rank of Lieutenant Commander. He was killed in an accident on June 15, 1932 when a Navy fighting plane piloted in a test by Commander Rodd crashed at East Camp, adjoining the naval base at Norfolk Virginia. He had made several landings and was taking off again when the aircraft's motor, according to observers, went dead at a height of 50 feet. Turning sharply, Commander Rodd was attempting to side-slip his plane to a landing when the dead motor suddenly opened up full throttle and the plane dived at full speed into the ground. He was buried with full honors at Arlington National Cemetery, section 7 site 9875.

> *Citation:* The Navy Cross is presented to Herbert C. Rodd, Lieutenant (j.g.), U.S. Navy (Reserve Force), for distinguished service in the line of his profession as a Member of the Crew of Seaplane *NC-4*, in making the first successful transatlantic flight. Date of Action: May 8–27, 1919

Eugene S. Rhoads

(August 20, 1891– April 1, 1975)

Eugene 'Smokey' Rhoads was born in Somerset, Pennsylvania town, on August 20, 1891. In 1905 he graduated from high school at the age of 14 and worked as a machinist until he wrangled a job firing on the Pennsylvania Railroad at age 16. He once shoveled 70 tons of coal on a 60-hour run. At the age of 18 he bumped into an old pal who had just joined the Navy. His pal assured Smokey that he had a good future in the Navy, for the grand sum of nine dollars a month with food, lodging and travel expenses thrown in. He then steered Smokey to the recruiting office. Smokey was toiling in the grimy innards of a battle-wagon when the word was passed for volunteers to join the Navy's budding aviation program and he ended up at Pensacola.

In those days, 1913, the Navy was running what amounted to a do-it-yourself flying service. Curtiss shipped the engines, hulls, and wing sections for the AH-8s to Pensacola and the Navy took it from there. Watching the AH-8, wheel out over the Gulf gave Smokey his first urge to fly, but the Navy was in no mood to make a flyboy out of a grease monkey. Besides, he was an enlisted man, flying was for officers.

So Smokey learned to fly on his own time and money. He shelled out his hard earned pay, taking lessons at a commercial field in Pensacola. He knew that if a young pilot wanted to live to be an old pilot a thorough knowledge of navigation was necessary, and that called for a math teacher. He found one in the person of a kindly nun in a Pensacola convent who agreed to teach him several evenings a week for five dollars a month tuition. "The fiver I spent in that convent gave me the best return I ever got for my money."

By the time the U.S. got involved in war with Mexico in 1914. Smokey was a pretty fair pilot, and although he wasn't an official Navy flier and was still toted as a machinist, he was granted permission to fly Navy planes. He was involved in the Mexican war and he said "For four months we flew all over the Mexican countryside on reconnaissance, buzzing the Bandito, scaring the hell out of their horses, and ducking rifle fire in return."

By 1916 he was back in Pensacola breaking what he considered the monotony of routine flying by testing some of the Navy's first parachutes. Toward the end of 1917 Smokey was ordered to Lands' End, England, to fly H- 16s on anti-submarine patrol over the English Channel. He left there in the summer of 1918.

Just prior to the time the war broke out Rodman Wanamaker had asked Glenn Curtiss to build the tri-motor America in an attempt to span the Atlantic to win the Daily Mail prize. Now the NC boats were to take over that role, and Smoky joined the division in time to watch the NC-1 test flights. He was assigned to the NC-4 under construction at the Garden City, Long Island plant.

After the famous flight Smokey left the Navy and spent time instructing New York's first flying police officers, and turned hundreds of Pensacola cadets into first-class flying men.

As late as 1950 when he was Chief Inspector of Naval Aircraft at Lockheed Aircraft in Burbank, California, Smokey Rhoads was known to finger the stick of the latest supersonic jet and kick it through its paces. Smokey died at the Veteran's Hospital, La Jolla Village Drive, San Diego, California on April 1. 1975.

Because of his outstanding achievements on the transatlantic flight of U.S. Navy Seaplane *NC-4,* on May 8 – 27, 1919 he was decorated with the Navy Cross.

> *Citation:* The Navy Cross is presented to Eugene S. Rhoads, Chief Machinist's Mate (Aviation), U.S. Navy, for distinguished service in the line of his profession as a Member of the Crew of seaplane *NC-4*, in making the first successful transatlantic flight.

From an article by Jack Goulding.

12

Gleanings

Contemporary writers' reports concerning events of the day provide additional interest. For this chapter several 1919 articles and other newspaper reports of later dates are reproduced. Some words on several reports gleaned from clipped newspaper scraps are missing from the scrap, this is indicated by ellipsis.

First we have an insider's view; part of an interview with Harry Town, a long-time Herreshoff employee who worked building the *NC-4* hull, and Albert E. Alder another retired Herreshoff employee; also an exchange of correspondence between the past curator of the Herreshoff Marine Museum and a collector of aircraft history.

The NC-4 U.S. Navy Flying Boat: Construction

In a 1969 interview, former Herreshoff Manufacturing Company employee Harry Town remembers details of building the *NC-4*. At the time of the interview Harry was the only man living who had worked building the*NC-4's* hull.

> Six men were assigned to build the hull. Ernest Alder was the foreman for the job. The hull was about 45-feet long with a 10-foot beam, and nicely rounded. The bare hull weighed only 2,800 pounds. The keel was of Sitka spruce, as was the planking. Expert craftsmanship for which Herreshoff was famous went into the project. The laminated hull had its double planking going 45-degrees forward and 45-degrees aft. To guarantee water-tightness and yet keep the planking thin, a layer of muslin in marine glue was set between the two plies.
>
> The hull's forward cockpit was open. Ash was steam bent and used to finish off the cockpit opening. The hull was copper fastened and was painted gray. The hull was shipped from the plant by railway.

A letter written by Albert E. Alder to *Yankee Magazine*, Dublin, N.H., March 7, 1979

In the March issue of *Yankee* there is an article [on a subject] very dear to my heart. It is the Navy–Curtiss *NC-4*. I think that the *NC-1* was built by the George Lawley & Sons, of Neponset, Mass. I do not know where the *NC-2* or the NC-3 was built, but the *NC-4* was built at the Herreshoff Mfg. Co. at Bristol, R.I. Her hull Number was Herreshoff 343. But officials at the Smithsonian say there are screw holes on the boat indicating it once had a plate but souvenir hunters took the plate.

On December 31, 1917, Mr. Ernest E. Alder, superintendent of the wood department was sent to the Glenn Curtiss plant on Long Island, N.Y., to get plans for a Navy super flying boat. I was with him on the trip. We were two days at the Curtiss plant, Mr. Alder came back to Bristol with all the blueprints. We were first to see the blueprints before anyone at the Herreshoff Mfg. Co., saw them.

On July 1, 1918, I went to work at the Herreshoff plant to learn the trade as a boat builder. During the building of the hull which became *NC-4*, I helped to do some of the work, and helped load the hull on the flat car at the N.Y.N.H.&H. [depot] in Bristol.

Very truly,
Albert E. Alder.

A letter from Albert E. Alder to Carlton J. Pinheiro, curator Herreshoff Marine Museum, April 25, 1979

Dear Sir;

I think that you were misinformed about the number of Flying Boat hulls that were built at the Herreshoff Plant during World War I. there were thirty (30) hulls, plus the *NC-4*. They were ten (10) called C-1, the other twenty (20) were called H-5-L. Mr. Norman Seymour and myself [*sic*] had charge of all the metal fittings that went on hulls of the F-5-L. All of those hulls were built in the north shop upside down, and were taken across the street to the east shop to be finished.

All hulls after they were completed were shipped to the Navy Yard at Philadelphia where the wings and motor was installed. No hull was completed at Bristol. The C-1 had one Liberty motor; the H-5-L had two Liberty motors.

The *NC-4* was built in what was the small boat shop. The end of the building had to be taken out in order to get the *NC-4* out. It was shipped by rail to Garden City, New York by New Haven Rail Road. I was one of the crew that helped to load the *NC-4* on the flat car.

Find enclosed a copy of the letter that I sent to *Yankee* about what I knew about the *NC-4*. Mr. Ernest E. Alder was with the Herreshoff Mfg. Co., for thirty-seven years and four months; he had a very keen memory.

The picture that you sent to *Yankee* of the flying boat was one of the four that was in Bristol for the 1919 4th of July celebration. All four boats were moored to the mooring buoys in front of the Herreshoff Plant. I have a picture of the same planes but taken at another angle.

I was very active, having worked on the first B-52 bomber also worked on the first after section of the 707 jet liner. I am seventy-eight years old; I was severely hurt in an elevator accident two years ago.

Yours truly,

Albert E. Alder

It appears from these letters that Albert E. Alder was the son of Ernest E. Alder.

A letter from Robert A. Gordon to Carlton J. Pinheiro past curator Herreshoff Marine Museum, May 7, 1979

Dear Mr. Pinheiro,

Thank you for copies of your correspondence on the NC and HS-2L flying boats. I have not run across the Herreshoff Manufacturing Company in researching the Gallaudet Aircraft Corporation. The George Lawley & Sons boatyard in Neponset, Massachusetts, was mentioned by a former Gallaudet employee and in one other source as the builder of at least some of the hulls for the Curtiss HS-2Ls, which Gallaudet produced. The ex-employee also named the Richardson Boat Works of Tonawanda, New York as a hull builder. It makes sense that at least two yards were involved since Gallaudet turned out a total of 60 HS-2Ls in something under one year's time.

If the number "1321" on the HS-2L in your photo was part of the U.S. Navy serial number (the complete serial number would have been A-1321), the particular aircraft was built by the LWF Engineering Company, Inc., of College Point, Long Island. LWF built the production batch with serials from A-1099 through A-1398. The serial number of the Gallaudet-built HS-2Ls was A-2217 through A-2276. Just as a guess, the four HS-2Ls moored off the Herreshoff yard may have been from the Navy base at Newport.

The Gallaudet Aircraft Corporation's plant was actually in Warwick [Rhode Island] on Chepiwanoxet Island Point. Gallaudet filled in the short distance to the mainland and turned a high-tide island into a peninsula. The mailing address was East Greenwich, probably because Chepiwanoxet was just across the Warwick town line and the East Greenwich Post Office was closer. It was down Alger Street off route 1. The old factory buildings survived until just a few years ago. They [the factory buildings] were being used as a marina in the mid-1960s when several CAHA members visited the site. They were eventually torn down to make room for, I believe, apartment buildings. Gallaudet built the plant in 1917, dropping out of aircraft manufacturing in 1929 and lasted a few years' longer building textile accessories before disappearing completely.

[Author's Note: if the writer continued his letter, it is now lost].

Associated Press May 16, 1919
Ponta Delgada, São Miguel, Azores
Azores Eagerly Awaiting Planes

Hundreds of natives crowd shores daily to see arrival of American planes. Harbor is Cleared of Craft to make Safe landing, and Destroyer are in Readiness.

Final preparations were made tonight to receive the American naval seaplanes, which are expected to arrive tomorrow, and the section of Ponta Delgada Harbor where the planes will be moored has been cleared of all craft to allow a safe landing. The weather, which was rainy and foggy today, is clearing tonight.

If the seaplanes follow the scheduled course they will first sight land at Corvo, of which is 300 miles west of Ponta Delgada. Supply boats have been stationed at Corvo and at Horta, on the southwest of the coast of the Island of Faial, in case of forced landing are necessary. Two destroyers are being held here in readiness to go to the assistance of the aviators if they are unable to find the harbor and they are compelled to alight on the open sea. All the destroyers are between the Azores and Lisbon are in position.

Intense interest in the flight is being manifested here, hundreds of persons crowding the waterfront daily awaiting the flyers.

Again, *NC-4* was forced to remain in harbor at Ponta Delgada, Ilha de São Miguel, Azores, waiting for favorable weather. While waiting for the weather to clear curious residents gathered for a close look at the Yankee flying boat. On May 27, the weather was good enough to resume the journey, and the crew once again took off, this time *en route* to Lisbon, Portugal.

New York Times, May 18, 1919

The progress of the Navy seaplanes on the transatlantic flight was put in table form tonight based on information as reported to the Navy Department in official dispatches. The *NC-4* time from Trepassey to Horta was 15 hours and 18 minutes, distance 1,200 sea miles.

The official dispatches give the progress of the flight in Greenwich Mean Time, but this has been reduced to New York time. The Navy Department was informed today that the corrected official starting time for the planes was:
NC-1—5:36 New York time;
NC-3—6:03 New York time;
NC-4—6:07 New York time.

	NC-1	NC-3	NC-4
Take off from Trepassey	5:36 p.m.	6:03 p.m.	6:07 p.m.
Out of sight	6:20 p.m.	6:20 p.m.	6:20 p.m.
Arrived Horta	9:25 a.m.	9:25 a.m.	9:25 a.m.

... speed of 22 knots, and the signal from the *NC-1* were getting stronger as the destroyer approached.

How far the destroyer was from the *NC-1* at that hour is not stated in the dispatch, but it was probably less than twenty-five miles, perhaps a great deal closer, as the *NC-1* when on the surface of the water has to fall down on its weaker sending radio set, which has a radius of only about twenty-five or thirty miles on the water. The more powerful radio set on the *NC-1*, which has a radius of several hundred miles under normal conditions can be used only when the propellers are working and when the craft is in the air.

The report from the USS *Columbia* (Cruiser No. 12) at Horta is telling of the success of the USS *Harding* (DD 91) in picking up the signals sent out by the *NC-1* was interpreted as meaning that the missing *NC-1* was somewhere north, northeast or northwest of the island of Corvo, and the fact that the radio signals from the *NC-1* were growing stronger as the *Harding* approached inspired naval officials with confidence that the plane would be found and rescued.

They were less concerned about the safety of the *NC-1* after receiving the message that they were over the whereabouts and safety of the other missing seaplane, the *NC-3* which had not been heard from since 5:14 o'clock this morning, Washington time or 9:14 Greenwich time. It was now daylight and that was an advantage for the *NC-3* but the fog, which interfered with the *NC-1*, had also to be faced by the *NC-3*, and deep concern was manifested over Commander Tower's plane.

The *NC-3* then was within 265 miles of the Port of Horta and had covered about 935 miles from the starting point in Trepassey Bay. The USS *Columbia's* message to the Navy Department, received at 8:45 o'clock tonight following which no other message had been received up to 19:30 o'clock Washington time tonight....

New York Times, Lisbon May 26 1919

FLIGHT-MAD LISBON LAYS HEAVY WAGERS
PLAN TO DECORATE FLYERS
Government Prepares Reception for *NC-4*
Spain Sends Invitation to Seaplane

Lisbon has a new forenoon sport—it is called listening for the sirens. Never did anxious Parisians listen more intently for the eerie wail that foretold the raid of German aircraft than the people of Lisbon for the steamer whistles lead by the cruiser U.S.S. *Rochester* and factory hooters, which will announce at noon one of these fine days that seaplane *NC-4* left Azores and again some hours later that her arrival at Tagus is due in sixty minutes.

Associated Press, Lisbon May 27, 1919

NC-4 LEAVES AZORES 6:18 A.M. OUR TIME
Arrives at Portuguese Port at 4:02 P.M.,
Averaging Over 82 Miles per Hour.

Start for Plymouth Today With Good Weather
Lisbon declaring a holiday and cheering thousands lining the shore greet the seaplane while bells ring and ship sirens shriek.

The achievement of the first transatlantic flight, with Lisbon as its first European stopping point has aroused the enthusiasm of the Portuguese as no event has stirred them in many years.

When the American seaplane *NC-4* came over the Tagus River this evening the population crowding all places of vantage gave full expression to the enthusiasm by cheers of welcome and booming of guns and the ringing of bells.

For days the people of Lisbon had been awaiting the completion of the momentous voyage over the Atlantic, and though disappointed from day to day because of the inability of Commander Read's craft to continue the flight from Azores because of unfavorable weather conditions, yet each day they looked hopefully to the west for the coming of the Americans.

Now they are able to say they never doubted that the *NC-4* would wing its way safely across the intervening 800 miles of water. Early in the day, word was flashed that the *NC-4* had started, and at intervals, there were bulletins of the progress made. The whole city was alert and during the later hours of the day virtually all businesses was abandoned by those who crowded everywhere to witness the arrival. Guided by skilful hands the American planes, which had covered the distance between the protecting destroyers along the route with clocklike regularity, swept on over Lisbon and settled down gracefully near the cruiser U.S.S. *Rochester*.

It was not forgotten by many of those who witnessed the triumph of the American commander that another man equally stouthearted, the Australian Hawker was being welcomed in England on his return from a wonderful trans-Atlantic flight more spectacular, but not so successful in its ending, and there was praise for both.

Associated Press, May 28, 1919

Plymouth, England Prepares for NC-4's Arrival
Mayor and Town Council of Plymouth to Extend Welcome.

Arrangements for the reception of Lieut. Commander A. C. Read and the crew of the *NC-4* when they reach this port, the end of the pioneer flight across the Atlantic, were completed today at a conference between the American naval authorities and the mayor. The only ceremony planned is for the mayor and the town council to extend a welcome to the aviators at the Mayflower Pier.

The American naval authorities believe the *NC-4* will arrive here Thursday or Friday. They expect the planes to enter the harbor here about 7 o'clock in the evening.

When the *NC-4* reaches the harbor a boat from the USS *Aroostook* will take off the crew and convey them to the pier. After the reception, the crew will be taken aboard the *Aroostook* where quarters have been provided for them.

New York Times, May 28, 1919

Schedule of *NC-4's* Eventful Flight
from Rockaway to the Portuguese Capital.

Washington, May 27 — the *NC-4* in its flight from Trepassey to Lisbon covered a distance of 2,150 nautical miles in 26.47 hours actual flying time or at an average speed of 80.3 nautical miles. The three seaplanes left Trepassey soon after noon on May 27, the eleventh day after its "hop" from Newfoundland. Its record in detail follows:

COURSE	DATE	DISTANCE	TIME	SPEED
Rockaway to Chatham Landing 10 miles off Chatham	May 8	300	5:45	52
Chatham to Halifax	May 14	320	3:51	85
Halifax to Trepassey	May 15	460	6:20	72.6
Trepassey to Horta	May 16–17	1,200	15:18	78.4
Horta to Porta Delgada	May 20	150	1:45	86.7
Porta Delgada to Lisbon	May 27	800	9:44	82.1
Complete ocean flight Trepassey to Lisbon		2,150	6.47	80.3

The *NC-4's* great flight began ominously;
Seaplane lost elevators in fire at Rockaway hanger
on evening of start.
She was crippled off Cape Cod, engine troubles in progress from
New York to the Azores.

The naval seaplane the *NC-4,* Lieutenant Commander Albert Cushing Read, U.S.N., commanding, which will go down in history as the first airplane to fly across the Atlantic, began the first leg of its transatlantic flight at the Rockaway Naval Air Station at 10 o'clock in the mooring of May 8 last. The day before it had narrowly escaped destruction in a fire, which damaged its elevators. It was the second of the three machines commanded by Commander John H. Towers to get underway on the long trip and was also first of the NC squadron to come (temporarily) to grief. Fortunately, for the record, the mishap occurred this side of Trepassey Bay, which was the official starting point of the flight, the result being with his arrival at Lisbon Commander Read had accomplished without mishap of any sort his officially mapped out course for the transatlantic air journey from Newfoundland to the Portuguese metropolis.

For the first six and one-half hours out from Rockaway Station all went well with the *NC-4*, which during that time kept its position in the squadron formation, the *NC-3*, flagship of Commander Towers leading the way, and the junior craft the *NC-1* and the *NC-4* following abreast, but off Cape Cod engine trouble developed, compelling Commander Read to alight in the open sea. The seaplane, however headed for Chatham under its own power until it was taken in tow a mile and one-half from that naval air station, On Wednesday, May 14 repairs again having been made, the *NC-4* resumed her flight to Halifax 340 miles distant, which she reached in safety, having average 98.6 land or 85 nautical miles per hour.

The *NC-4* remained in Halifax for one day, and at 9:03 A.M., on Thursday, May 15 started for Trepassey to rejoin the other two seaplanes, which had reached there in the meantime.

Twenty-six miles out, however, further trouble with the engines occurred, and the *NC-4* taxied back to Halifax. At 11:46 A.M. she went into the air for the second time and arrived at Trepassey Bay 5:41 P.M., May 15. The *NC-3* and the *NC-1* had made an effort to start the Azores part of the flight....

... *Rochester* and factory hooters, which will announce at noon one of these fine days that seaplane *NC-4* left Azores and again some hours later that her arrival at Tagus is due in sixty minutes.

On the principal squares and in the cafes as the mid-day approaches one sees people looking at their watches and comparing the time. For not only are the Portuguese intensely interested in American flight and delighted that their capital has been chosen as the point of arrival, but they are also inveterate gamblers and large amounts of money change hands each noon, according whether the *NC-4* started or not.

Last night a Portuguese captain with French-British war crosses staked at evens [even money] $500 he had just gathered from the [roulette] wheel that the *NC-4* would be floating in the Tagus before tomorrow night.

This morning the *New York Times* correspondent was assaulted by a group of Portuguese University students, who would let no barrier of language interfere with their determination to know the exact details of the *NC-4*'s adventure.

The American warships here are not idle during the period of waiting for the seaplane *NC-4*. Admiral Plunkett informed the *New York Times* correspondent that he has instructed the destroyers to locate and blow up with machine gun fire two floating mines reported by Portuguese sailing ships in the neighborhood of the Tagus mouth. The first was reported about only three-miles from the station of the destroyer *MacDougall*, just outside the estuary, the other was some fifty-miles northward.

In addition to the enthusiastic welcome planned by the Portuguese government—including the decoration of the airmen with one or two of the highest honors in the country, the Order of Christ dating back six centuries, comparable to the Spanish Golden Fleece, and the Torre Espada—the Tower and Sword nearly less ancient. I learned today that the Spanish authorities have telegraphed the American Naval Chief at Paris for the permission for the seaplane to visit Port Ferrol, where they are planning a reception to rival Lisbon's.

Bristol Phoenix October 3, 1919

The Boat of the Famous Craft was made at Herreshoff's

The big naval flying boat the *NC-4* the hull of which was built by the Herreshoff Manufacturing Company of this town flew over Bristol Wednesday afternoon about 3:15 o'clock on its trip from New Bedford to Providence, Lieutenant Commander Albert C. Read in command. A trip to boost recruiting in the [U.S.] Navy air service from Maine to Florida began last Saturday, starting from Portland. The *NC-4* arrived at Boston at 3:45, and remaining until Wednesday morning when the seaplane flew to New Bedford, remaining six hours before starting for Providence.

Besides Lieutenant Commander Read, the crew of the *NC-4* included Lieutenant Walter Hinton pilot; Lieutenant H. C. Rodd, radioman; Ensign P. Talbot, Chief Boatswain's Mate; Daniel Moore, Chief Machinist Mate; C. I. Kessler and C. S. Rhodes Chief Machinist Mates.

Lieutenant Hinton and Ensign Talbot took turns at the steering wheel in the flight to Providence. Lieutenant Hinton was the man who actually piloted the *NC-4* on her famous trip across the Atlantic. Chief Machinist Mate Moore was on the *NC-1* and repaired the engines three times while in flight in mid-ocean.

The flying boat passed directly over the plant of the Herreshoff Manufacturing Company on the trip to Providence, Wednesday afternoon. Flying at a low altitude the seaplane was seen by thousands along the route. The powerful Liberty motors made a tremendous noise.

The hull of the *NC-4* built at the Herreshoff's is 45-feet long and about 10-feet abeam. It is of cedar, one-eighth of an inch thick strengthened by canvas While the hull was

View of the Navy-Curtiss *NC-4* flying boat visiting Atlantic City, New Jersey in September 1919. At the time the airplane, was participating in a recruiting tour. *[USN]*

The *NC-4* always draws a large crowd no matter where or when. This crowd of curious citizens is making a close up inspection of the plane in New York's Central Park on July 13, 1919. *[USN]*

In this view the *NC-4* is taxiing to its mooring on a visit to Atlantic City, New Jersey in September 1919. At the time the airplane was participating in a recruiting tour.

being built here it was known as the *NC-1* but after it had been shipped to the Curtiss Aeroplane Corporation where the frames for the wings were made and the machine put together it was renamed the *NC-4*.The Curtiss Corporation officials considered the hull built here as the best of the lot, and it is of course a source of satisfaction to the local firm that their boat was the first to be carried across the Atlantic in an air flight.

Yesterday a parade of naval men was given in Providence in the interest of recruiting.

Bristol Phoenix May 9, 1969

Bristol men present at *NC-4* commemoration

Two men who helped build the *NC-4*, the first plane to cross the Atlantic Ocean were on hand in Washington, D.C. yesterday to help commemorate the 50th anniversary of the historic flight. T. P. Brightman and Harry Town, who helped construct the body of the plane at the Herreshoff Mfg. Co., in 1918–19 were invited guests at ceremonies sponsored by the U.S. Navy and the Smithsonian Institute. Mr. Brightman and Mr. Town, along with the editor of the *Phoenix* [Roswell Bosworth, Sr.] were in the large audience, which heard of the *NC-4's* exploits including stops at St. Michael's in the Azores and Lisbon. Their participation was through the efforts of Senator John O.

In June 1923, during the Shiner's Washington, D.C. convention the *NC-4* was displayed on the Washington Monument grounds where a tourist took this snapshot.

A November 18, 1919 snapshot of a crowd of sightseers viewing the *NC-4* on the Paducah, Kentucky waterfront.

Pastore. A number of local men were involved in building the 45-foot body of the plane and one Bristol man, the late Charles Callan was in the ground crew of the NC group. [Bristol resident] Admiral Gilbert C. Hoover, then a lieutenant witnessed the flight from a battleship, which served as a surface patrol ship for the flight.

13

An Address by Carlton J. Pinheiro

On Friday evening, December 4, 1998, Carlton J. Pinheiro, past curator of the Herreshoff Marine Museum addressed the Bristol and Ponta Delgada Rotary Clubs on the subject of the *NC-4*. Pinheiro's talk is presented here through courtesy of the Herreshoff Marine Museum.

This museum celebrates the yachts and accomplishments of the Herreshoff Manufacturing Company, internationally known for the building of many America's Cup Defenders. This evening however, I am not going to speak about these sailboats, but about another of our proudest products—the *NC-4* seaplane.

Eighty years ago, An American plane, the *NC-4* became the first plane to fly the Atlantic. The people of Bristol take pride in the fact that the Herreshoff Manufacturing Company played a major role in contributing to the successful flight. Over the years, a Bristolian has carried the torch for the *NC-4*, making certain in his newspaper that we would never forget that great accomplishment. That Bristolian is of course Rotary President and [Bristol] *Phoenix* publisher Ros[well] Bosworth, Jr. We, here at the Museum and I, in particular, will with his permission, now take that torch from him to insure that the saga of the *NC-4* is never forgotten.

Generally, when Americans are asked who made the first transatlantic flight, they will quickly reply that Charles Lindbergh did so in the *Spirit of St. Louis*. An Englishman will tell you that Alcock and Brown did in a Vickers-Vimy biplane, and like most Americans will also be incorrect.

The first plane to fly across the Atlantic was the U.S. Navy's *NC-4* flying boat, which crossed from Newfoundland to Lisbon, Portugal with stops in the Azores Islands in May of 1919. Later in 1919, Alcock and Brown made the first non-stop flight; Lindbergh made the first solo Non-stop [flight] in 1927. The flight of the *NC-4* was conceived in August 1917 when Rear Admiral David W. Taylor of the Bureau of Construction and Repair decided that for anti-submarine work the Navy needed a Large sea-based patrol bomber that would be capable of flying directly to the theater of war in Europe instead of using valuable shipping space [to transport the aircraft].

Glenn H. Curtiss, pioneer aviator the "father" of the aerial flying boat, and head of the Curtiss Aeroplane and Motor Company, was called in as a consultant to work out details. In January 1918, the Navy gave Curtiss a contract for four NC (Navy–Curtiss) flying boats. The components of the aircraft were manufactured by several subcontractors and assembled at the new Curtiss plant at Garden City, Long Island. The *NC-1* was completely built and assembled at the Curtiss plant but the hulls and pontoons of *NC-2* and *NC-3* were built at Lawley's boatyard in Neponset, Massachusetts. The hull and pontoons for the *NC-4* were built at the Herreshoff Yard in Bristol, Rhode Island.

With the end of the war in Europe on November 11, 1918, there was no longer a need of these huge expensive flying boats. On the preceding October 31, however, Commander John H. Towers proposed to the Chief of Naval Operations that the NC boats [should] be prepared to fly the Atlantic before the summer of 1919. Several routes were examined and it was determined that the NC flying boats did not have range enough to fly nonstop from Newfoundland to Ireland or England. The flight would therefore have to be made by way of the Azores and Portugal.

The role of the Herreshoff Manufacturing Company in the *NC-4* saga began on December 31, 1917, when Ernest E. Alder, superintendent of the wood department was sent to the Glenn Curtiss plant on Long Island to get plans of a Navy flying boat. Accompanying Mr. Alder on the trip was his teenage son, Albert. After spending two days at the Curtiss plant, the Alders returned to Bristol with all the blueprints needed for hull construction.

In 1979, Albert Alder, then, 79 years old, recalled that he worked on the hull in 1918 when he went to work at the yard and helped to load it on the railroad flatcar at the Bristol train depot, when it was shipped to New York. He recalled that, "The hull was built in the small boat shop and the end of the building had to be taken out on order to get the hull out." Another man on the construction crew, Harry Town, told [me] that the hull was double planked on mahogany with muslin and shellac between the two layers. The hull bore the bronze plate of the Herreshoff makers and was numbered Hull 341.

The biplane hull was 45-feet long, with a beam of 10-feet. It had a 126 foot wingspan (4-feet shorter than a Boeing 707). The total length from nose to the tip of the tail was 68-feet, 3½-inches. It was propelled by four Packard Liberty engines. Three engines pulled and the fourth pushed the *NC-4* through the air at about 80 to 90 miles per hour.

The flight of the big Navy flying boat began on May 2, 1919, but it took the *NC-4* a total of 26 days to make the trip to Lisbon. The *NC-2* was taken apart for [spare] parts for the *NC-1*, so only 3 flying boats made the initial takeoff from Newfoundland after leaving Long Island, New York. The *NC-1* and *NC-3* had difficulty on the flight to the Azores. Because of fog, the *NC-1* touched down [on the sea] but could not take-off again in the bad weather. The waves destroyed enough of her hull to eventually cause her to sink. Luckily her crew was rescued.

The *NC-3* also put down at sea, but the shock [of hitting the surface] buckled the struts supporting the center engines. Although no longer able to fly, she continued on the surface and ended her journey at Ponta Delgada, San Miguel, in the Azores.

For almost 3 days, the *NC-4* was at her moorings at Horta, kept there by the terrible weather. On May 20, there was enough clearing to allow the flying boat to take-off. In less than two hours, she reached Ponta Delgada on the island of San Miguel. [Commander] Read planned to leave for Lisbon the next day, but the weather delayed his departure for another week, finally leaving for Lisbon on May 27.

At twilight on the same day, the Capo da Roca Lighthouse toward the Tagus Estuary was sighted—the westernmost point in Europe. The *NC-4* turned southwest toward the Tagus Estuary and Lisbon. At 2001-hours on May 27, 1919 the *NC-4* touched down on the waters of the Tagus. The first transatlantic flight was fact. After two days in Lisbon where all three NC crews were generously received by the City of Lisbon and the Portuguese government, *NC*-4 departed Lisbon. A few hours later she was forced down at the river at Figueira, had repairs and continued to El Ferrol, Spain for the night. The next day *NC-4* made the final leg of the monumental flight and landed in the harbor of Plymouth, England in the afternoon of May 30.

Men would fly the Atlantic again and again. The route of the *NC-4* became the model for Pan-American flights. Planes became faster, making fewer stops, fly with more passengers and at speeds no one could ever have imagined in 1919.

The honor for that remarkable flight belongs to Lieutenant Commander Albert Cushing Read, his crew of five, the United States Navy's *NC-4* and the Herreshoff Manufacturing Company of Bristol, Rhode Island.

But no one again would ever be FIRST.

Hundreds of citizens inspect the massive *NC-4* during the Navy's east coast recruiting effort, using the flying boat as a draw.

14

Overview of Significant Events

May 8, 1919—*NC-1, NC-3,* and *NC-4* Take off from Jamaica Bay at Far Rockaway, Queens for Halifax, Nova Scotia. During flight the *NC-4* develops engine trouble off Cape Cod and diverts to Chatham Massachusetts. The *NC-1, NC-3* arrive at Halifax without incident.

May 10, 1919—*NC-1, NC-3*, continue to Trepassey Bay, Newfoundland.

May 14, 1919—*NC-4*, flies to Halifax and arrives at Trepassey Bay the next day.

May 16, 1919—*NC-1, NC-3,* and *NC-4* leave Trepassey Bay, Newfoundland, for Horta, Azores Island.

May 17, 1919—*NC-4* arrives at Horta, Azores Island. *NC-1* lands at sea and sinks 3 days later. Its crew is picked up by the Greek freighter, the *Ionia*. *NC-3* is badly damaged after landing near Horta.

May 19, 1919—*NC-3* battered and almost derelict sails into Ponta Delgada Harbor.

May 27, 1919—*NC-4* leaves Horta and arrives at Lisbon, completing the first American transatlantic flight.

May 29, 1919—*NC-4* leaves Lisbon for Plymouth and diverts to El Ferrol, Spain due to engine trouble.

May 31, 1919—*NC-4* arrives at Plymouth, England.

U.S. Coast Guard Aviator number 1, Lt. Walter Stone is often forgotten by Navy buffs as a Coast Guardsman. The Naval Reservists (USNRF) was often not mentioning their Reserve status: this means they did not go to the Naval Academy, but were on active duty all the same; i.e., regular college graduates or commissioned from the ranks.

Eugene Rhoads was a Chief Machinist's Mate (Air) as opposed to a surface Navy (ship) machinist. In the early days of aviation, they were sometimes called by the French word MECHANICIAN. Chief Petty Officers feel slighted if the "Chief" is left off. Rhoads name is often misspelled; Rhoads is correct.

The NCs were so highly regarded that for decades all US aircraft registrations began with "NC."

After the first Atlantic crossing, the *NC-4* made a tour of eastern and southern U.S. cities.

In 1922, the remaining NCs became P2Ns, although this designation was not used.

The Curtiss NCs' original tri-engine plan was redesigned with four engines for the trans-Atlantic flight.

The *NC-4*, long-range flying float plane is preserved by the Smithsonian Institution, which restored it in 1969.

Power supply: four 400-hp, Liberty V-12 liquid-cooled piston engines
Total horsepower: 1,600
Max speed: 74 knots, minimum speed: 58 knots
Endurance: 14 hr. 8 min at cruising speed
Climb rate: 2000 ft. in 10 minutes
Ceiling: 2,500
Fuel capacity: 1,841 gallons
Capacity oil tanks: 160 gallons
Weight: empty 15,874 lb., gross 28,000 lb.
Crew: six
Span upper wing: 126 feet
Span lower wing: 94 feet
Wing area: 2,380 square feet
Length: 68 feet, 5½ inches
Height: 24 feet, 5⅛ inches
Wing area: 2,442 square feet

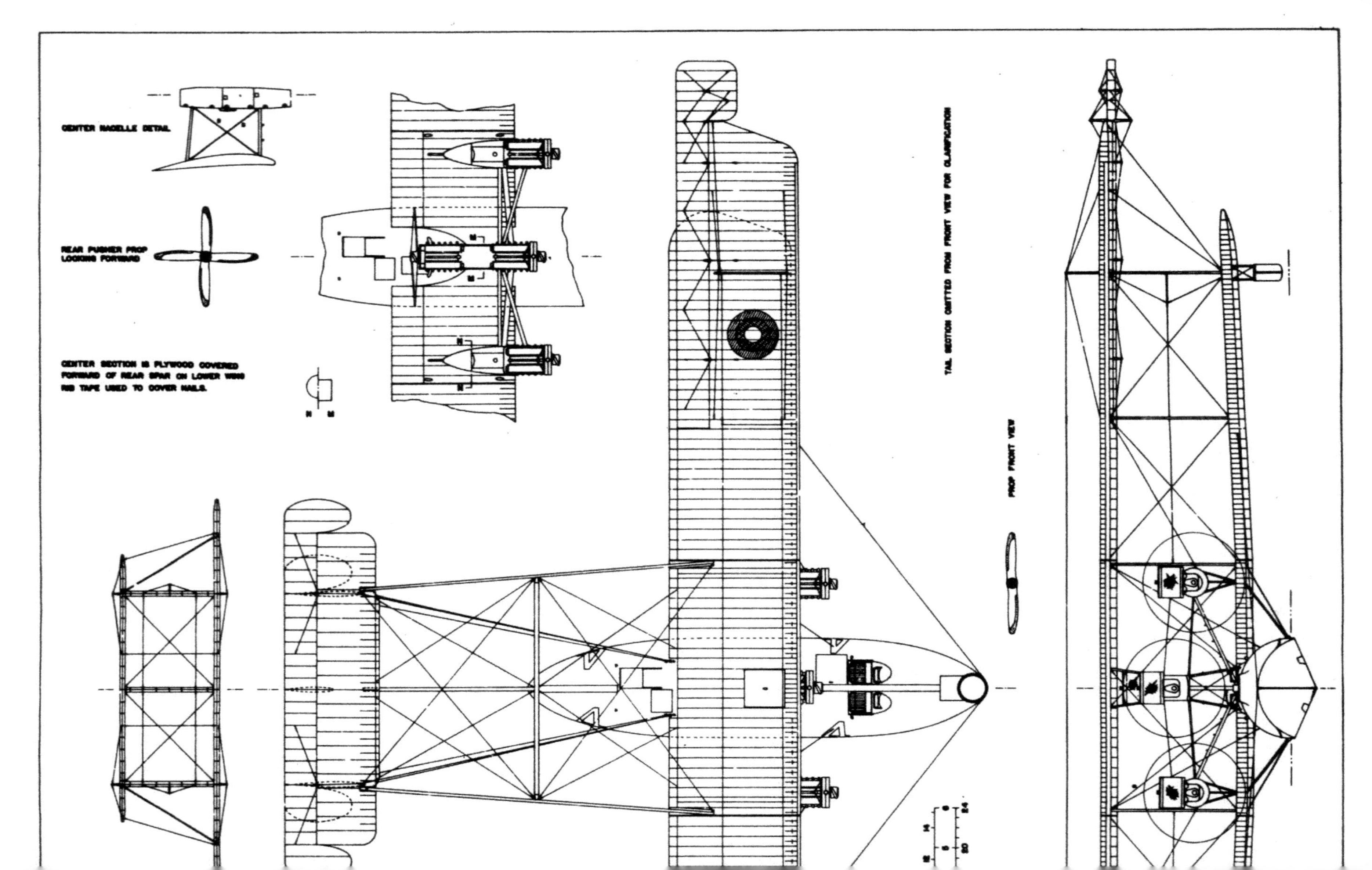

CENTER NACELLE DETAIL
REAR PUSHER PROP
LOOKING FORWARD
CENTER SECTION IS PLYWOOD COVERED
FORWARD OF REAR SPAR ON LOWER WING
RIB TAPE USED TO COVER NAILS.
TAIL SECTION OMITTED FROM FRONT VIEW FOR CLARIFICATION
PROP FRONT VIEW

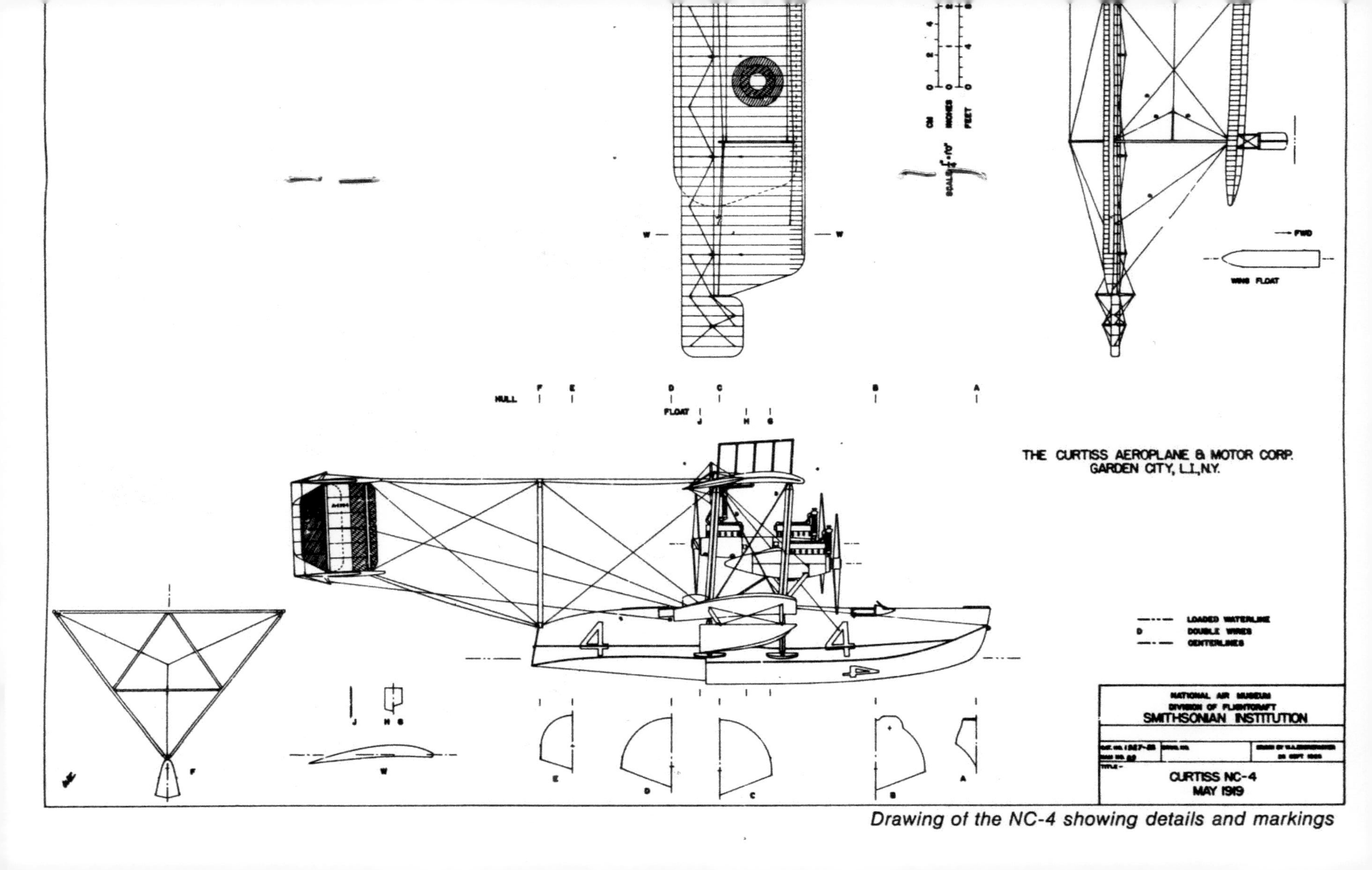

Drawing of the NC-4 showing details and markings

Everywhere the Navy exhibits the *NC-4* during the Navy's recruiting drive hundreds of citizens, young and old, line up for a chance to touch a flying boat.

15

Restoring the Nancy Boat for Public Display

An essay by J. O. C. James Johnston, Courtesy of *Aviation News*

The *NC-4* was in the beginning for pioneer glider pilot Paul Garber a matter of professional interest, but in the years ahead, it became an obsession.

Garber, recently [1969] retired assistant director of the National Air and Space Museum first saw the flying boat at Rockaway Naval Air Station during the time of its preparation for the transatlantic flight. He was a young man then with the air postal service. The next time he saw the *NC-4* it had returned from Europe and was on display in New York's Central Park.

"I saw it twice in Washington, once in Anacostia, once on exhibit at the Washington Monument and one other time in Philadelphia," he recalled.

Throughout his years at the Smithsonian Institution, where he first went to work in 1920, Garber retained his enthusiasm for aircraft. When World War Two broke out, Garber was commissioned in the Navy. By this time, he had begun efforts to have the *NC-4* brought to the National Air Museum for preservation and display. He was unable to maintain clause contact with the Smithsonian Institution during the war, but he did try to keep track of the *NC-4*, which he believed was stored at the Naval Gun Factory. He learned however that it was in Norfolk and on a trip there, he visited the naval base to inquire about it.

"I found the airplane in a storage area in Norfolk," he said, "and a chief petty officer told me the buildings were being emptied and the contents would be moved elsewhere."

Garber, by this time desperate to salvage the famous flying boat, asked for an appointment with the base commander. By great good fortune, the Norfolk commander at the time was Rear Admiral Patrick N. L. Bellinger, who had been the pilot of the *NC-1*.

The admiral of course agreed with Garber that the *NC-4* should be preserved and ordered the parts stored in a new location at Cheatham Virginia. The seaplane remained in Cheatham until Garber after the war arranged to have it moved to Washington and subsequently to the Air and Space Museum's Preservation and Restoration Branch in Silver Hill, Maryland. The flying boat's hull was displayed in the museum in 1920, but its size and the lack of facilities precluded display in its entirety.

None the less, the restoration branch five years ago [1964] began restoring the airplane for eventual display in a new Air and Space Museum still being planned. Priority projects eventually pushed the *NC-4* restoration into the background until two years ago [1967] when with the 50th anniversary of the flight approaching, the Navy and the Smithsonian decided to refurbish the plane for display this summer [1969].

The *NC-4* again took precedence in the restoration division with the full crew devoting it entire time to the flying boat—no small task.

Chief of restoration and preservation branch at Silver Hill Donald K. Merchant says, "The *NC-4* is the largest project we have ever undertaken to date, and quite probably it is the largest we will ever attempt."

Working over a two-year period on the engines alone, two men at Silver Hill have restored the four Liberty V-12s to mint condition. To do this they disassembled the engines and rebuilt them.

At the same time, two other men were working on the wing sections. The *NC-4* surface covers an area of more that 4,785 square feet. Each section was stripped down and recovered with imported Irish linen, which is about identical to the original material. Then three coats of dope were applied and finally six coats of color pigmentation were sprayed on.

The doping was perhaps the most frustrating aspect of the restoration. Humidity and temperature ranges for proper tautness and drying are critical—humidity of 40 to 50 percent in room temperature preferably 72 degrees. Therefore, the doping process frequently was delayed while the technicians awaited proper conditions. Additionally, each wing section has an average of 1,000 knots of rib stitching, all hand sown.

Simultaneously, but in another section of the Silver Hill hanger another group of technicians worked on the hull. The 40-foot boat was reinforced from the inside with doublers and given three coats of gray paint. From the waterline up it was recovered with fabric over the wood. About 70 feet of new rubber walkway was installed on the hull and on the angled engine struts.

Most of the cockpit had to be reconstructed from the instrument panels to the upholstery on the seats and around the cockpit.

The work was progressing but the anniversary date—May 8—was rapidly approaching and there was still much work to do on the flying boat. The Navy and Smithsonian Committee with Commander C. A. E. Johnston, the Navy project coordinator requested that three Navy enlisted men from NAF Washington be assigned to the NC project to help manufacture small parts and put the airplane together. The three men began working at Silver Hill in a temporary additional duty status. By March, the restoration was nearing completion.

The [Navy] technicians' first fitted the lower center wing section to the hull to insure proper seating. Then the wing assembly was carried out in another hanger since none of the buildings at Silver Hill was large enough to accommodate the entire built-up flying boat. Starting with the center section, the four Liberty engines were slung. Then the outer panels, struts, cables and wires were fitted. Assembly took the crew the better part of a week.

The sections were disassembled for transportation downtown—about a ten-mile drive for final reconstruction on the mall near the Air and Space Museum.

That the success of the *NC-4* flying boat marked a monumental milestone in the progress of world aviation is undeniable. Yet, it was this plane of which it was said a little more than 50 years ago [1919]: "the machine ... is impossible and is not likely to be of any use whatever."

16

A Gallery of Early U.S. Navy Float Planes and Flying Boats

FREE INSTRUCTION IN THE OPERATION OF THE

CURTISS FLYING BOAT

WILL BE GIVEN TO THOSE TAKING A REGULAR COURSE OF TRAINING AT

The Curtiss School of Aviation

SAN DIEGO, CAL.

One of many Curtiss School of Aviation advertisements appearing in many national magazines and newspapers—this one is in the December 7, 1912 issue of *Aero and Hydro*. The illustration is of the first race between hydroaeroplanes. Glenn Curtiss is in the lead at the control of his "Flying Boat."

Above and below: Launching and testing a Curtiss hydroaeroplane ordered by the U.S. Navy; it is of the same type as the flying boat *America. [Aero and Hydro magazine photo, 1912]*

The U.S. Navy's first aviator Lieutenant Theodore G. Ellyson sits beside Glenn H. Curtiss of the early hydroaeroplane as they prepare to take off in 1911 from Keuka Lake, Hammondsport, N.Y. Ellyson's career was tragically cut short in 1928 when the plane he was piloting crashed into Chesapeake Bay.

The hull of this Curtiss H1-6 flying boat was built by the Herreshoff Manufacturing Company of Bristol, Rhode Island, *c.* 1918.

Curtiss designed H-16 flying boats with hulls built by Herreshoff at the Naval Air Station seaplane apron Pensacola, Florida, *c.* 1918. Also seen in the center distance are HS-11 seaplanes. *[U.S. Naval Historical Center photograph]*

This is one of 20 F5L flying boat hulls built by the Herreshoff Mfg. Co. *c.* 1927. *[U.S. Naval Historical Center photograph]*

Another view of the H-16 flying boat, *c.* 1922. Notice the similarity to the *NC-4* in the placement of the navigator and pilots' cockpits. *[USN]*

Tent hangers on the beach housed seven flying boats and hydroaeroplanes moved from Annapolis to Pensacola in 1914. The first aviation unit numbered only nine officers and 23 men. During World War Two the Pensacola flying school trained thousands of Navy pilots. Notice the "pusher" type engine on the plane in the foreground.

A Curtiss F-5L drops a 1,000 pound dummy torpedo in tests conducted by the Naval Aircraft Factory, Philadelphia, PA, on November 28, 1918. The factory in the background appears to be the Hog Island shipyard. *[U.S. Naval Historical Center photograph]*

The submarine S-1 launches a Cox-Klemin XS-2 seaplane off the coast of New London, CT, *c.* 1926. The plane was carried, disassembled, in a waterproof tank on the submarine's deck.

A Navy float plane test drops a MK-7 torpedo in Newport (RI) Harbor, *c.* 1920. *[Naval Torpedo Station photo]*

Left to right: Lt Walter Hinton, pilot; Lt E. F. Stone, U.S. Coast Guard; Ensign Howard C. Rodd, radioman; Lt James L. Breese, engineer; Chief Machinist's Mate Eugene S. Rhodes; Lieutenant Commander Albert C. Read and Admiral Dominick Arnold Jackson.

A single engine flying boat throttles up for a takeoff from the U.S. Naval air station, Hampton Roads, VA. Notice the "bull's eye" wing insignia, which dates this photo to about 1920.

APPENDIX A

Richard E. Byrd

While organizing the base in Canada, Lt. Byrd worked with Lt. Hinton on the transoceanic problems. Hours were spent charting courses and plotting requirements until all that was needed was the big *NC-1* itself. But Washington's silence on the subject during the fall of 1918 was nearly as ominous as the increasing frequency of the coastal storms. With the armistice, Byrd's dream came crashing down. The Allies' victory had wrecked his hopes. Closing his stations and sending his men back to the States, he headed for Washington, and then during his trip south he heard the transatlantic flight was still on, after all. Upon arrival in the capital, his spirits were further buoyed when he heard that his friend Commander Towers was going to be in charge of the operation, The "Great Hop" was going forward surely there would be a place for him.

Then, came the next report, "No officer or man who has had foreign duty will be permitted to be a member of the transatlantic flight expedition. This includes those who have been on Canadian detail."

The first blow came when he heard that the Navy's Director of Aviation Captain N. E. Irwin was sending him back to Pensacola. This was too much—he went to see the Director. There is no record of the ensuing conversation between Lt. Byrd and Captain Irwin, but the young officer's argument must have been persuasive because in February 1919 Byrd joined the transatlantic Flight Section in Washington.

APPENDIX B

U.S. Navy contracts with the Herreshoff Manufacturing Co.

Date	Owner	Length/Type	Boat's Name
1879	U.S. Navy	28′ Steam Cutter	Dolphin
1879	U.S. Navy	100′ Steam Cutter	Inca
1880	U.S. Navy	42′ Open Launch	Spray
1881	U.S. Navy	57′ SPAR Torpedo Boat	Lightning
1884	U.S. Navy	94′ SPAR Torpedo Boat	Lucile
1890	U.S. Navy	138′ Sea-going Torpedo Boat	Cushing
1892	U.S. Coast Survey	23′ Tender	Wasp
1893	U.S. Navy	28′ Steam Launch	Enterprise
1895	U.S. Coast Survey	28′ Tender	Eagle
1897	U.S. Navy	175′ 6″ Sea-going Torpedo Boat	Dupont
1897	U.S. Navy	175′ 6″ Sea-going Torpedo Boat	Porter
1898	U.S. Navy	100′ Sea-going Torpedo Boat	Gwin
1898	U.S. Navy	140′ Sea-going Torpedo Boat	Morris
18i98	U.S. Navy	100′ Sea-going Torpedo Boat	Talbot
1898	U.S. Navy	33′ steam Launch	Atlanta
1890	U.S. Navy	40′ Rescue Boat	
1892	U.S. Navy	83′ Ferry/Water Cannon Boat	Wave
1896	U.S. Navy	54′ 3″ Steam Cabin Yacht	Javelin
1900	U.S. Coast Survey	26′ Tender	Yankton
1902	U.S. Navy	Ten 58′ Steel Barges	
1902	U.S. Navy	Twenty F-5-L Flying Boat Hulls	
1903	U.S. Coast Survey	27′ Tender	Patterson
1903	U.S. Navy	29′ 5½″ Steam Launch	Ladoga
1905	U.S. Navy	Five 40′ Torpedo Retrievers	C3365-C369
1909	U.S. Fish Commission	26′ 3″ Launch	Albatross
1914	U.S. Navy	30′ Launch	Vixen
1918	U.S. Navy	Ten H-16 Flying Boat Hulls	
1918	U.S. Navy	Flying Boat Hull	NC-4
1929	U.S. Army	45′ Launch	Kanawa
1932	U.S. Coast Survey	28′ Launch	Yosemite

Endnotes

Introduction

1 USS *Columbia* (Cruiser # 12, later CA-16), 1894–1922. She was briefly named *Old Columbia* in 1921–1922; a 7,375-ton protected cruiser built at Philadelphia, Pennsylvania, she was commissioned in April 1894.

Chapter 1

1 USS *North Carolina* (ACR-12) was a Tennessee class armored cruiser of the United States Navy.

Chapter 2

1 Theodore Gordon Ellyson, USN (February 27, 1885–February 27, 1928), nicknamed "Spuds", was the first United States Navy officer designated as an aviator "Naval Aviator No. 1."

Chapter 4

1 It is worthy to note that the hulls did survive constant slamming into the ocean, it was the engines which most often failed and the fragile wings that collapsed under stress.

Chapter 5

1 Engine problems forced the *NC-4* to return to Chatham where it stayed until May 14.

Chapter 6

1 Cape Cod to Halifax: four ships; Halifax to Trepassey: four ships; Trepassey to Azores: twenty ships; Azores to Lisbon: thirteen ships; Lisbon to Ferrol: five ships (the so-called A, B, C, D and E ships); Ferrol to Plymouth: five ships. Some references disagree with the number and names of station ships.

2 The USS *Aroostook* (CM3) was the Eastern Steamship Company's *Bunker Hill* converted for planting mines during the First World War.

Chapter 7

1 A barbican is a fortified outpost or gateway, such as an outer defense to a city or castle, or any tower situated over a gate or bridge which was used for defense.

Chapter 8

1 The Isles of Scilly are an archipelago off the southwestern tip of the Cornish peninsula of Great Britain.
2 The Spanish American War-era Protected Cruiser USS *Baltimore* (C3).
3 North Atlantic Marine Group.
4 DD67 *Wilkes* a destroyer which served during the First World War.
5 The USS *Melville* (destroyer Tender No. 2); commissioned December 3, 1915.
6 After the Armistice, the *Rochester* served as a transport bringing troops back home. In May 1919, she served as flagship of the destroyer squadron guarding the transatlantic flight of the Navy's NC seaplanes.
7 USS *Tarbell* (DD-142) was a Wickes-class destroyer in the United States Navy during the First World War. She was the first ship named for Captain Joseph Tarbell.
8 USS *Harding* (DD-91) was a Wickes-class destroyer in the United States Navy serving during the First World War.
9 USS *Biddle* (DD-151) was a Wickes-class destroyer in the United States Navy; Biddle was launched October 3, 1918, and commissioned April 22, 1919.
10 USS *Stockton* (later DD-73), 1917–1940. In May 1919, during the transatlantic flight of the *NC-4* aircraft, she was stationed on plane guard duty west of the Azores.
11 The USS *George Washington* (ID-3018), was a German ocean liner, launched in 1908. She was taken over and converted into a transport by the US Navy during the First World War. She was sold for scrap in 1951.
12 The USS *Hannibal* (AG-1) is a converted steamer, built at Sunderland, England, in 1898. She was purchased by the United States Navy on April 16, 1898. She was one of the very few ships to serve in the US Navy in the Spanish-American War and both World Wars.
13 The Cattewater is that stretch of water where the mouth of the River Plym merges with Plymouth Sound, just to the east of Sutton Pool.

Bibliography

Note on Sources

The text, photographs, and illustrations used in this narrative: *The U.S. Navy–Curtiss Flying Boat NC-4*; concerning the world's first transatlantic flight are from diverse sources, the author has made every effort to identify those sources.

Illustrations are from contemporary periodicals, period post cards, sightseers' snapshots and official US Navy photos released for public information. Generally, text is from early-to-late twentieth-century commercial books, scientific journals, newspaper clippings, technical magazines and pamphlets some of which are in the public domain.

For brevity, all official U.S. Navy photographs are known by this identifier [USN].

'Aero and Hydro', *Aeronautical Magazine*, December 7, 1912.

Bellinger, Patrick N. L. VAdm USN, 'Sailors in the Sky'; *National Geographic*, August, 1961

Bowers, Peter M., 'Tale of the Nancy Boats', *Flight Journal*, August 1999.

Jardee, Jack, *Flight of the NC-4*, Sea Classics, 2011.

Lucev, Emil R., *The Great Flight,* The Wave of Long Island, May 1986.

Popular Science, May 1946.

Sears, Stephen W., 'The Intrepid Mr. Curtiss', *American Heritage*; April 1975.

Smith, Richard K., *First Across*, United States Naval Institute, 1973.

Tillman, Barrette, 'The Fleet is Born', *Flight Journal*, April 2011.

Wesiberger, Bernard A., 'First to fly the Atlantic', *American Heritage*, June 1969.

Wilber, Ted (Commander USN), 'The First Flight Across the Atlantic', *Naval Aviation News*, May 1969.

About the Author

Richard V. Simpson is a native Rhode Islander who has always lived within walking distance to Narragansett Bay; first in the Edgewood section of Cranston and in Bristol where he has lived since 1960. A graphic designer by trade, he worked in advertising, printing, display, and textile design studios. He designed and built parade floats for Kaiser Aluminum's Bristol plant and the Navy in Newport; he painted large murals for Kaiser, Raytheon's Submarine Signal Division, and outdoor billboards depicting U.S, Navy Supply Corps history for the Naval Supply Center in Newport.

After retiring in 1996 from a 29-year Federal Civil Service career with the US Navy Supply Center and Naval Undersea Warfare Center in Newport, he began a second career as an author of books on subjects of historical interest in Rhode Island's East Bay, with his principal focus on Bristol. This is Richard's twenty-fourth published title, the third with a military theme as its subject. Beginning in 1985, he acted as contributing editor for the national monthly *Antiques & Collecting Magazine* in which 85 of his articles on antique and collectable subjects have appeared.

Bristol's famous Independence Day celebration and parade was Richard's first venture in writing a major history narrative. His 1989 *Independence Day: How the Day is Celebrated in Bristol, Rhode Island* is the singular authoritative book on the subject; his many anecdotal Fourth of July articles have appeared in the local *Bristol Phoenix* and the *Providence Journal*. His history of Bristol's Independence Day celebration is the source of a story in the July 1989 *Yankee Magazine*, and July 4, 2010 issue of *Parade Magazine*, and an interview on National Public Radio.

Books by Richard V. Simpson

A History of the Italian-Roman Catholic Church in Bristol, RI (1967)
Independence Day: How the Day is Celebrated in Bristol, RI (1989)
Old St. Mary's: Mother Church in Bristol, RI (1994)

Publisher: Arcadia Publishing

Bristol, Rhode Island: In the Mount Hope Lands of King Philip (1996)
Portsmouth, Rhode Island, Pocasset: Ancestral Lands of the Narragansett (1997)
Tiverton and Little Compton, Rhode Island: Pocasset and Sakonnet (1997)
Tiverton and Little Compton, Rhode Island volume II (1998)
Bristol, Rhode Island: The Bristol Renaissance (1998)
America's Cup Yachts: The Rhode Island Connection (1999)
Building the Mosquito Fleet: U.S. Navy's First Torpedo Boats (2001)
Bristol: Montaup to Poppasquash (2002)
Bristol, Rhode Island: A Postcard History (2005)
Narragansett Bay: A Postcard History (2005)

Publisher: the History Press

Herreshoff Yachts: Seven Generations (2007)
Historic Bristol: Tales from an Old Rhode Island Seaport (2008)
The America's Cup: Trials and Triumphs (2010)
Tiverton & Little Compton Rhode Island: Historic Tales (2012)
Quest for the America's Cup: Sailing to Victory (2012)
Historic Tales of Colonial Rhode Island (2012)

Publisher: Fonthill Media, LLC

Preserving Bristol: Restoring, Reviving and Remembering (2014)
Thomas J. Lipton's America's Cup Campaigns (2015)
Bristol Through Time (2015)
The U.S. Navy–Curtiss Flying Boat NC-4 (2016)
Goat Island and the Naval Torpedo Station (2016)